SPEAK TO ME!

Public Speaking as Enlarged Conversation

Second Edition

Melinda S. Womack, Ph.D.
Santiago Canyon College
Rancho Santiago Community College District

KENDALL/HUNT PUBLISHING COMPANY
4050 Westmark Drive   Dubuque, Iowa 52002

Dedication

WILLIAM GEORGE WOMACK
1930 - 1997

To Billy; professor, co-author, colleague, mentor, best friend, soul mate, husband, lover and gift from the Heavens. His 40 years of experience with public speaking was the cornerstone of our first edition of this textbook and remains the backbone of this second edition.

Billy understood my shyness. I offer unending thanks to him for insisting I go to lunch with Jeanne M. Walker, Ph.D. The completion of this second edition following Billy's death is due, in large part, to Jeannie's presence. Both my willingness and ability to get on with my life are directly related to her continual guidance, support, laughter, humor, unrestricted access to both her office and home (with a praiseworthy and most inspiring patio), and our "once in a lifetime," God-given friendship, that shall last a lifetime.

To Billy and Jeannie, my soul-felt thanks.

Table of Contents

Introduction:
To the Student and Instructor

This text is the product of over 40 years-combined experience in teaching public speaking. Instructors have continually struggled with balancing theory and practice within the constraints of the college semester/quarter. I have used countless public speaking texts—most of which have left me frustrated—either because they overemphasize theory (leaving skills buried between the lines) or overemphasized skills (leaving the impression that the art of public speaking is merely a list of behaviors to assume). Because of this **Speak to Me! Public Speaking as Enlarged Conversation** is a text that, I believe, realistically reflects what can and needs to be accomplished in the typical course in public speaking.

Speak to Me! can be used as the primary text in either a beginning or intermediate public speaking course. Instructors are strongly encouraged to add their own materials and experience to supplement this text and "make the course their own." The text was written with this in mind.

I believe that **Speak to Me!** addresses issues in a natural order of learning. The first chapters cover the personal concerns, including critical thinking and cultural diversity issues, and the public speaking process. Succeeding chapters emphasize how to develop a speech. The final chapters focus on specific types of speeches. The chapters are written to stand-alone. Because of this, you may find repetition of information. Since repetition is one of the most powerful tools for learning, I have made a conscious effort to incorporate this as often as is reasonable. Due to the stand-alone quality of the chapters, instructors may deviate from the printed order without loss of continuity.

Written in "enlarged conversational" language, this textbook models the approach I take with public speaking. I will be engaging, therefore, in "conversation" with you, the reader, throughout our journey toward the understanding of and competence in public speaking.

Four major changes have occurred with the writing of the second edition. Attention has been given to cultural diversity, critical thinking, the role of the audience, and exercises implementing the application of theory to everyday life. Each of these areas needs to be addressed at this point.

About Cultural Diversity

Public speaking is indigenous to Western civilization -- the roots of public speaking are found in ancient Greece. The reality of our world today is civilization rich in diversity. The public speaking classroom is both blessed and challenged by this multi-cultural reality. Public speaking taps into our culture's firmly held belief in individualism. How does this affect those students identifying with a collectivist culture? How do these identities affect an individual's subsequent communication style and effectiveness?

It is not within the scope of this text to instruct students in the area of intercultural communication nor to provide thorough background in the area of culture. This text does challenge, however, both the student and instructor to raise issues of cultural diversity as they pertain to the public speaking process. To this purpose, Chapters 1 through 6 include a section at the end of each chapter raising cultural diversity issues to be addressed -- either individually or as a class.

Author's View of Culture

I need to present my view of culture. Understanding my perspective will guide you toward a better understanding of my writing.

What is culture? Culture is a "learned set of shared perceptions about beliefs, values, and norms, which affect the behaviors of a relatively large group of people" (Lustig & Koester, 1996, pg. 41). Ethnicity or nationality does not limit culture, therefore. Rather, culture includes as well, broadly defined groups defined by Western and Eastern perspectives, and gender, as well as relatively smaller groups of individuals defined by generation, organization, or peer group. As students and instructors, we must embrace the reality that today, more than any other time in history, our classrooms are rich in diversity -- and, therefore, rich in challenge.

My hope is that we embrace our differences and learn to communicate with them -- rather than insist on melting down our cultures into one "melting pot" identity. As Julia T. Wood (1999) states in her book, *Gendered Lives: Communication, Gender, and Culture*:

> Perhaps it is time to abandon the melting pot metaphor and inaugurate a new one that acclaims difference as valuable and desirable, one that remakes the cultural ideal to incorporate all citizens instead of trying to remake diverse citizens to fit a single, noninclusive ideal ... To create a new vision, we must realize that we participate in a common world, yet each of us experiences it somewhat differently from standpoints

shaped by intersections among gender, race, class, and affectional preference (pg. 385).

About Critical Thinking

Since, at least, the influence of Socrates and Aristotle in ancient Greece, oral communication has been noted as an essential element in the furtherance of knowledge and decision-making. I cannot imagine a college course in public speaking *not* addressing this issue. Throughout the text, including the entire Chapter 1, which is devoted to critical thinking in public speaking, I challenge both the speaker and the audience to incorporate critical thinking skills into the preparation, delivery and interpretation of the public message. A section is included at the end of Chapters 1 through 6 that raises critical thinking issues to be addressed by both the speaker and the audience.

Applying the Text to Your Life

No course in communication is worth the time and effort unless you, the student, can apply to your own life the knowledge of both the communication process and effective communication behavior. I bring in day-to-day practical application of the public speaking principles throughout the text. At the end of Chapters 1 through 6, I supply practical application for the particular areas covered in each chapter. Chapters 7 through 13 are devoted to practical applications in the public speaking setting.

The Role of the Audience

The role of the audience is often assumed to be understood yet we rarely are given guidance as to how to behave as the critical element in the communication process. Chapter 5 devotes attention to this very issue specifically focused on audience participation in the public speaking classroom. Included in this chapter are discussions about rhetorical sensitivity, communication styles and types, and dialogue.

I hope you find **Speak to Me!** a practical yet thought provoking approach to the teaching and learning of public speaking. Enjoy the journey that ends in conversing with the public in a formalized setting.

About the Author

I am a tenured professor of Speech Communication at Santiago Canyon College, Orange, California. I also teach communication courses at Chapman University and within the California State University system. I received my Ph.D. degree in Communication Arts & Sciences from the University of Southern California.

I have taught Public Speaking, Interpersonal Communication, Group Dynamics, Business Communication, Oral Interpretation and Gender Communication for 15 years. The Rancho Santiago College District (of which Santiago Canyon College is a part) has awarded me the Distinguished Faculty Lecturer," "Publication," and, "Professional Achievement" awards.

Chapter 1: The Power of Speech - Critical Thinking

ritical thinking is a term that often creates semantic noise. Over the years, I have listened to many students who perceive critical thinking as a difficult, cumbersome, "brainy" task with no real benefit except, maybe, college credit. The purpose of this chapter is **not** to provide a comprehensive discussion of critical thinking, rather the purpose is to highlight the process and illustrate the importance of critical thinking in the public speaking communication process from the perspectives of both the speaker and the audience.

Definition of Critical Thinking

Critical thinking is intelligent reasoning with supporting evidence to help make wise decisions. Critical thinking is finding support to substantiate your behavior, choice, position or idea. Another term for critical thinking is reflective reasoning. The opposite of reflective reasoning is reactive thinking. Reactive thinking means that an individual makes a decision without considering the consequences. Is this always negative? What about spontaneity?

Definition of Reactive Thinking

Spontaneity, or reactive thinking, occurs when we act or make decisions without consideration of the consequences. Again, is this always negative? No—as long as the personal worth and safety of those involved are not jeopardized. A component of the creative process is spontaneity. As communication, including public speaking, is grounded in spontaneity—are we as public speakers at fault for not incorporating critical thinking at all times? This is a delicate balance and a primary concern for the public speaker. The act of public speaking is most often "planned spontaneity." That is, with careful preparation the public speaker communicates in the "here and now" with the audience. The effect is that through preparation the public speaker has engaged in enlarged conversation with the audience.

When is spontaneity negative? This is the time to begin our discussion on the concept of **situations that matter**. Situations that matter occur when the personal worth and/or safety (mental, emotional or physical) of those involved is in jeopardy. In other words, situations that matter put personal worth and safety in direct relationship with the consequences of the situation.

At a minimum, public speaking involves two situations that matter: (1) the speech development process and (2) the actual speaking event. This, of course, brings us back to the concept of ethics as presented earlier in the section titled, **To the Student and Instructor**. These issues will be further discussed in the next section, **Why Critical Thinking in Public Speaking**.

Why Critical Thinking In Public Speaking?

In her text, *Second Thoughts: Critical Thinking from a Multicultural Perspective*, Wanda Teays writes:

> One of the tasks of critical thinking is to enable students to approach issues, assess evidence, examine assumptions, sort out moral, legal, and social considerations, and arrive at decisions. In order to do this well, we must have a receptive and reflective disposition or be guided by a desire for truth and fairness. (1996, pg. vii)

She also writes:

> An educated citizenry is at the heart of the true democracy. People who can think critically cannot be manipulated into believing lies are truth. The entire jury system depends on people being able to tell the difference between assumptions and facts, between fallacious reasoning and well-supported arguments. "Misinformation campaigns" work only when we fall for them, when we accept unsupported claims and tolerate sloppy thinking. (1996, pg. 3)

So, why critical thinking in public speaking? Because without critical thinking in public speaking, we are putting ourselves into the position of being manipulated by other's whims and/or good intentions. The point being -- we turn over our lives to those exherting influences when we do not incorporate critical thinking.

Power

Public speaking is about power. Klopf defines power as "the ability to determine the behavior of others, even against their will" (1998, pg. 169). I disagree. Klopf's definition puts both the impetus and decision for power in the hands of the person requesting the power. The relational, or transactional, view of communication presents power as co-defined. That is, while an individual may request power (e.g., "stop smoking," "turn left at the next intersection," "purchase this particular car"), power does not exist until the other individual(s) acts upon the request (e.g., the individual stops smoking, turns left at the next corner, or purchases the car).

So, whether we are speaking or listening to messages of influence (to change, continue, or adopt a behavior; to understand, or to respond emotionally) we are always a responsible party to the decision of whether or not power will exist. Both the public speaker and the individuals in her audience are responsible for the influence gained by the speaker for that particular speaking event.

Ethics and Responsibility in Public Speaking

This brings me to the discussion of ethics and responsibility in the public speaking process. When a person stands in front of an audience and participates in the communication process with that audience, both speaker and audience take on a tremendous responsibility. Responsibility refers to accountability.

As audience members, we seem to assume that the speaker is there for our best interests. In addition, in the pure sense of democracy and ethics (dealing with what is right and wrong), speakers should be communicating with us in the best interest of everyone involved. Nevertheless, we know, by personal experience and observation of other events, that there are unethical speakers -- communicators with only self-interest or limited interest in mind. Where does the ethical responsibility lie? On the shoulders of the speaker or the audience? The answer is both.

As speakers, we are responsible to our audience not to violate their trust. We are in a position of potentially great power -- the United States culture praises those who are competent public speakers (promotion, celebrity, leadership, etc.). As you will discover in future chapters, communication does not just involve words, but by necessity, incorporates the intellectual and emotional (and sometimes, spiritual) energies of those involved. To violate these energies is unethical -- wrong -- by democratic standards. This means we must approach our audience members with the best information possible with solid reasoning and appropriate choices -- no matter what the purpose of the public speaking event.

As audience members, we are responsible to ourselves to be prepared to not "tolerate sloppy thinking" (Teays, pg. 96). If we are uneducated about and/or unwilling to test solid reasoning, we are to blame for allowing ourselves to be influenced by the speaker in ways we regret. **The speaker and the audience, therefore, co-define the outcome of a public speaking event.** If the outcome is positive -- we all get credit. If the outcome is negative -- yes -- we all get credit.

Tools for Critical Thinking

The two available tools for incorporating the critical thinking process are reasoning and evidence. Reasoning is the drawing of inferences or conclusions using explanation, justification or logical defense. Evidence is something that furnishes proof. Confused? Stay with me. When we think, we make sense of our world (explanations, justification, logical defenses) by coming to conclusions (drawing inferences) based on what we perceive as real (proof/evidence). Reflective reasoning (critical thinking) tests the validity of our evidence, conclusions and the subsequent consequences of our actions based on those conclusions. Reactive thinking (spontaneous, noncritical thinking) does not consider the evidence, conclusions or consequences.

Types of Reasoning

When we reason well, we make certain that conclusions logically flow from the original premise, or, that which we assume or take for granted. Logic is not to be confused with truth because false premises can trick us. For example, there was a time when we believed that the sun revolved around the earth -- after all, we could see it in the eastern sky in the morning and watch it as it traveled toward the western sky throughout the course of the day. Logical? Well, we held that belief for centuries. This belief is still very much a part of our language (e.g., "sunrise" and "sunset"). Not until we had access to more information did we discover that we were operating on two false premises: (1) the sun orbits, and (2) the earth is stationary. Lessons: Even the most obvious may not be truth, and, we cannot assume we see or know all there is to see and know. So, we do the best we can with what we have and search for the most truthful explanation possible.

There are two basic types of reasoning; inductive and deductive. While distinct from one another, they are not opposites.

Inductive reasoning involves drawing a general conclusion from pieces of evidence. We are asked to infer meaning -- to pull together a complete picture based on bits of information, or evidence. A crime scene provides a perfect example. Detectives arrive at the scene of the crime. They collect evidence -- fingerprints, footprints, blood samples, photographs of the scene are taken, times are noted, and witness statements are collected. Based on this evidence, the legal system attempts to reconstruct the crime and solve the "whodunit" mystery. How accurate is this? You tell me. In a court of law, the very same body of evidence will be interpreted by the defense and the prosecution to come up with conclusions of not guilty and guilty, respectively.

Deductive reasoning involves drawing a conclusion from general premises. For example, our court system often operates on the premise that the birth mother is necessarily the best guardian for the child. My very dear friends are foster parents to two beautiful children who were temporarily removed from the custody of their birth mother because the mother was fighting a long battle with drug addiction. In the eight months these children have been with their foster parents, they have become physically healthy, more social, they want to go to school, and they report that they never have been happier. My friends want to adopt these children but the courts keep delaying the process because the birth mother has the right to take them back at any time -- in spite of the fact that her addiction is getting worse. In addition, she is consciously making no attempt to get help and she admits to willful abuse of the children and an unwillingness to seek help. Is the birth mother the best guardian? Many say "no." Now, the courts say, "yes." What is the truth in this situation?

Incorporate critical thinking in situations that matter. Test that the premises are valid. But validity of premise is not the final test. In addition to validity, be certain that the premises are cogent. Reasoning is cogent if it is justified, based on valid reasoning and premises, and founded upon relevant information, or evidence.

Types of Evidence

There are three general types of evidence; facts, testimony, and statistics. A fact is something that is provable. Equally important, a fact is something that cannot be disproven. Testimonial evidence includes statements of opinion and experience by reliable expert witnesses. Statistical evidence involves the use of numbers for the purpose of prediction.

Each of the three types of evidence has inherent issues of fault. Basing conclusions on facts would seem most desirable with the least room for error. True enough. Except that we must always question whether we have sufficient facts, facts that do account for the complete issue, and facts that are, indeed, facts -- not opinion. Testimony is faulty in that witnesses are subject to personal biases and perceptual inaccuracies inherent in the human perception system. Always question the reliability and expertise of witnesses. Statistical data is based on averages from samples. All statistics, no matter how well collected, are inherently limited.

So, how do we come to know the truth if our only means of investigation are inherently faulty? By gathering as much evidence as possible, from as many perspectives of the issue as possible, and continually measuring our conclusions against our reality as we know it. Not a simple answer by any means.

As public speakers, we must test our conclusions against our evidence before ever presenting our information to the audience. As audience members, we must not blindly accept a speaker's conclusions -- rather, we must weight the speaker's messages against our own critical thinking measures.

Oh, my. It is true. Your worst nightmare is coming true. You really do have to make a speech in this class! The instructor has just announced that the first round of speeches begins next class session:

P A N I C !
What will I talk about?
Why am I shaking?
I feel so nervous before I've even begun!
How can I get out of this?
When is the next flight to Tibet?
Am I the only one feeling so scared?

You are not alone! In fact, congratulations! You are normal!

Modern research show that only about 5% of the population reports low anxiety when confronted with the need to speak in public. These same studies show over 70% of us report moderate to high anxiety when we speak or even think about speaking publicly (McCrosky & Richman, 1980).

Even experienced professional actors and speakers report speech anxiety. Mark Twain (Samuel Clemens) once said, "The fright that filled me from head to foot was paralyzing. It lasted for a full two minutes." Sir Winston Churchill, former Prime Minister of Great Britain, when asked if he ever experienced speech fright said, "Yes. Each time before a major speech I feel like I have a block of ice nine inches by nine inches by nine inches around my middle." I have been an instructor of public speaking for over 15 years and I am a professional actor. I still experience what I have come to know as normal nervousness before speaking (and performing), but it took many speaking experiences before I understood and came to accept the "butterflies" as a normal, positive sign.

My goal is to help you understand what speech anxiety is, why it happens and how to cope with the feelings. This three-step process will help you to turn speech "fright" into speech "might."

What is Speech Fright?

Our reaction to public speaking is the same reaction we have to any stress situation. We experience a "cascade of chemicals" released through the adrenal glands which causes our body to be in a "super alert" state ready for "fight or flight." What we call speech fright is a set of physical and mental symptoms:

- ❏ Pounding heart
- ❏ Shaking hands or knees
- ❏ Dry mouth
- ❏ Shallow breathing
- ❏ Loosing control
- ❏ Forgetting
- ❏ Quavering voice
- ❏ Blocking
- ❏ SYSTEM OVERLOAD

If we interpret our physical symptoms to mean loss of control, panic and terror, we will often find ourselves thinking:

I'm out of control!
I can't do this!
I'm so embarrassed!
I'll just die!

The symptoms get worse.

If, however, we interpret our physical symptoms as normal reactions to a stress situation, we find ourselves thinking:

I feel up!
I'm okay!
My nervousness doesn't show much!
I get better as I speak!
I look better than I feel!
I'll do fine!

The symptoms reduce and we feel in control.

The result of the two different interpretations of the same set of symptoms is enormous. If you interpret your speech fright symptoms as a loss of control or falling apart, the result will be increasing:

Panic
Mind blanking
Terror
Blocking

Feelings of disaster

If you experience the speech fright symptoms as normal nervousness, as feeling "pumped up," as a temporary condition, the result will be increased:

Energy
Positive nervousness
Short term symptoms
Ability to proceed
Feelings of competence

You can make this choice. While you may have established reaction habits, you can learn new reactions to similar situations. This takes time, but it can be done.

Why Does Speech Fright Occur?

We know through the research of Arnold Buss (1984) that we have eight reasons to fear speaking in public.

1. We tend to have more speech fright in novel situations. For most of us, speaking in public is not an everyday event.
2. We experience more speech fright in formal situations. Many of us have been taught to see public speaking as rigid, rule-bound and formal.
3. We experience speech fright when we are in a subordinate position. If we see our audience as superior and dominant, we feel subordinated.
4. Our speech fright increases when we feel conspicuous. Public speakers are definitely conspicuous!
5. We experience heightened speech fright when dealing with the unfamiliar. When we are unfamiliar with the material we cover,

the audience and even the place at which we speak, we tend to experience more speech fright.

6. Speech fright escalates with the degree of attention we receive from others. We do not like to be stared at or ignored.

7. Evaluation will increase our anxiety or speech fright. Our fears tend to grow if we perceive the audience to be our judge rather than a group of people who wish to hear what we have to say.

8. Speech fright can be reinforced. If we have a prior history of what we see as failure, we will likely fail again. On the positive side, however, the same principle works with success: Each successful speech predicts more success.

Practical Suggestions for Coping with Speech Fright

First, get the idea of performance out of your conception of public speaking. **The purpose of public communication is to share ideas, present new or important information, to show the need for change, to uplift or inspire, or to lighten the mood of the audience with a humorous treatment of any topic. Public communication is to _EXPRESS NOT IMPRESS_.** The public speaker is neither an actor nor an interpreter of literature. When we speak to an audience we have the task of sharing, of focusing on our material in such a way that the listeners understand, learn, change or simply relax and enjoy.

By keeping our mind focused on the audience and on our material we change our perception away from self and keep it on our receivers; onto our message and away from self. This is the beginning of freedom from speech fright.

- ❏ Stay idea centered
- ❏ Analyze your audience not yourself
- ❏ Understand public speaking as enlarged conversation

13

The following partial list of suggestions will help you systematically rethink your idea of public speaking:

- Accept your fear. You are normal. The anxiety can be accepted, managed, and used to make you a better speaker.
- PREPARE! Proper preparation will reduce speech fright by nearly 80%.
- Choose a topic you already know something about.
- Choose a topic that means something to you.
- DO NOT MEMORIZE WORD FOR WORD.
- Develop a positive metaphor for public speaking. Examples: Public speaking is enlarged conversation. Public speaking is just sharing my thoughts and feelings. Public speaking is leading a guided tour of my idea. Public speaking is my gift of ideas/feelings to others.
- Visualize yourself speaking to friends.
- Keep your attention focused on the audience and your ideas.
- Stay informal, when appropriate. Although a speech may have elements of the formal, try to find ways to relax. Sit. Take off your jacket. Ask questions.
- PRACTICE!
- Know it is okay to have an occasional lapse of memory. If this happens, acknowledge it and move on (you do this every day in conversations).
- BE BOLD (or appear bold)!
- Use your face; smile, frown. Use your body, arms, and hands. This energizes you and the audience. In addition, using your body helps spend some of that stressful energy.
- PRACTICE! Talk to a friend.
- Show you are happy to be there.
- Show you are interested in your listeners and your topic.
- PREPARE!

- Organize the topic into 3 main sections: Example:
  - Topic: Self (introduction speech)
  - Part One: Self as student
  - Part Two: Self as worker
  - Part Three: Self as parent
- Plan a conclusion.
- Plan an introduction
- PLAN!
- Rely on logical, natural sequence of ideas or events to guide you.
- Stay IDEA centered (the words will come as you think about each natural part of the speech).

These suggestions have, and do, work for beginning as well as advanced speakers. The secret is not to expect immediate results. Converting speech "fright" to speech "might" takes time and practice. This course is designed to enhance your public communication through awareness of public speaking techniques and allow you time to **PLAN, PREPARE,** and **PRACTICE.**

Diversity Issues Regarding Speech Fright

1. With which cultures are you most comfortable communicating? Why?
2. With which cultures are you least comfortable communicating? Why?
3. Spend time communicating with a member of your public speaking class who identifies with a culture different from yours. Ask that individual to answer questions 1 and 2 above. Compare your answers with one another. What have you learned? How might your answers affect the communication within this particular class?

Critical Thinking Issues Regarding Speech Fright

1. The next time you are experiencing speech anxiety, make note of the particular "fear scenario" you imagine (e.g., "I'll lose my job if I make a mistake," or, "everyone will laugh at me"). What evidence do you have to claim those conclusions as valid?
2. Do you believe speech anxiety to be based in reflective or reactive thinking? What implications does your answer generate regarding the nature and focusing of your speech fright?

Exercises: Applying the Chapter to Your Life

1. Speech anxiety can be expressed in any communication context. Whenever you feel awkward or want to avoid speaking in any situation, jot down as much as you can remember regarding:
   - With whom and where were you speaking?
   - When?
   - Why? What was the purpose of your interaction?
   - Topics discussed
   - Emotions involved
   - Was this a prepared or spontaneous interaction?

   Each list will give you insight. Collect as many as you can and then look for trends. This may indicate to you where your speech fright "triggers" exist.

2. Force yourself to speak publicly at least once every week. Suggestions include:
   - Prayer
   - Introduction
   - Input at a meeting
   - Make an announcement
   - Request information

Note your progress regarding your communication comfort after the third week. If your symptoms are getting worse, consult with your public speaking instructor for guidance.

Chapter 3: Enlarged Conversation - The Public Speaking Process

The purpose of this chapter is to give you an understanding of the overall process of human communication as it pertains to the public speaking context. We will look at the various models of communication, including a careful look at the transactional model, and the individual components of the model as they apply specifically to public speaking.

Why Is it Important to Know about the Process of Human Communication?

What is happening when we converse with another person (interpersonal communication) or when we speak with an audience (public speaking)? I believe it is critical for the communicator to have a realistic model of the communication process because from this model comes the way the communicator thinks about and reacts to those involved in the process.

Several models of the communication process are available. Because it is simple to understand, some people choose as their guide the stimulus-response, or sender-receiver, (S-R) model. This model is also known as the linear or mechanistic model. The S-R description of communication in the public speaking context looks like this:

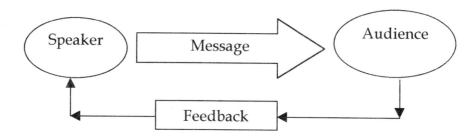

If we choose to use this communication model it will limit our understanding by conceptualizing the speaker as active stimulus with an audience of passive receivers into which the speaker pours information: Speaker talks, the audience listens. Speaker stops and the audience provides comments through questions or comments about the message. Simple? Yes! Realistic? No!

The Transactional Model

There is a more realistic and helpful communication model available. This model is called the transactional perspective. As a transactional process, communication is understood to be a **simultaneous creation**: Both participants in the communication event are simultaneously sending and receiving messages, therefore, simultaneously acting as stimulus and response. The transactional model for public speaking looks like this:

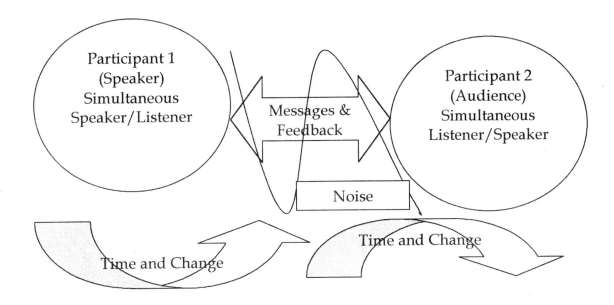

In addition, this perspective takes into account the personalities (thoughts, feelings, perceptions) of the participants in the process, namely, the speaker and the audience members. Both participants (speaker and audience) are experiencing changes in their perceptions or understandings at the same time and on many levels.

The communication process works this way: Both the speaker and the audience members simultaneously encode and decode (send and receive) messages through noise that effect the individuals over time and create change in perceptions and behaviors (communication).

I believe that the transactional model does describe what happens in the process of public speaking. Both the speaker and each individual listener are encoding and decoding verbal and nonverbal cues, simultaneously: Both are sending and receiving messages at the same time.

When you understand public speaking this way, you begin to see that the speaker and all of the listeners are involved in a form of one-to-one transaction. In reality, the public speaker is in conversation with each member of the audience. Just as we do in our daily conversation, we adjust our words and nonverbal messages to one member of the audience at a time and each audience member simultaneously and independently responds. From this transactional model, you begin to see how the title of this text was a natural evolution. Enlarged conversation is a practical way to describe/conceptualize what is actually happening when we speak with an audience. The additional element, however, is that while speaking one-to-one, the situation still involves communicating within a public context with a group consisting of individuals yet psychologically still having to deal with the dynamics of both interpersonal and group processes (See Chapter 5, **The Role of the Audience**).

Whether conscious or not of the transaction, most successful public speakers operate from a transactional perspective. The effective speaker is a spontaneous co-creator of the message as she communicates with "individual" audience members.

Speech content and delivery change as necessary for understanding; eye contact will be individualized to each person for a few seconds before moving to the next person. The speaker will be aware of the constant nonverbal feedback from each person and aware of cross talk between audience members as he speaks. Because of this perspective, the public speaker knows it is possible, and even preferred, to adjust content and delivery so the individuals in the audience best decode the message. This takes us back to my original metaphor: **Public speaking is, at its best, an enlarged conversation.**

Even the manuscripted speech reader can learn to adjust to the transaction occurring in public speaking by ad-libbing, that is, departing from the prepared remarks. An effective manuscripted speaker will be able to decode the needs of her audience and meet them by sharing, for example, a nonscripted story, dropping or adding points of information, bringing in some aspect of the communication situation (heat, cold, time, etc.) or by referring directly to an individual in the audience for emphasis on the transaction.

Key Elements of the Public Speaking Transaction

The essential elements of the public speaking transaction are:

- **Encode**: To create the message mentally—word and nonword forms.
- **Sending**: Creating physical signal (communication behavior; e.g., verbal and nonverbal).
- **Receiving**: A neuro-physical activity involving perception and processing of sensual signals. In face-to-face communication, the primary sense signals are visual and auditory.
- **Decode:** To interpret signals received from word and nonword forms—to attach meaning.
- **Speaker-Sender (Participant):** While a participant in the communication process, the speaker-sender is the primary encoder in the public speaking setting.
- **Message:** Both the intended information sent and the received information decoded.
- **Noise:** Any element that distorts the understanding of the message, in either sending or receiving.

- **Delivery:** The use of verbal and nonverbal signals to send the message while following a specific speech delivery format, or method.
- **Listener(s)-Receiver(s) (Participants):** In the public speaking setting the audience is the primary listener. The audience participates in the communication process, however, by simultaneously receiving and sending messages.
- **Feedback:** The message, either verbal or nonverbal, that follows the original message.
- **Situation/Setting:** The context wherein the speaking event takes place.

It is useful to look at each element or aspect of the communication process in order to understand this ever-changing, unfolding phenomenon we take so much for granted.

Speaker-Sender (Participant)

We start with the thoughts, ideas, feelings, attitudes and needs within us as speakers which urge us to communicate. It has been said that we do not make a speech—the speech makes us. The ideas, feelings, attitudes, values and needs we have internalized, and the changes we are involved with **drive us** to communicate. One important idea will generate millions of words. The effective public speaker is idea-centered.

The encoding process is the intellectual act of selecting symbols coupled with the physical act of producing sound and visual signals which change into understandable public speech (sending). We do this everyday in every conversation in which we take part: We put into words and physical expressions what is bothering us, what we need, what happened to us, or what we think. We ask questions or persuade a friend to give us a ride home or excitedly share the plot of a movie we have seen. We encode all of this, almost automatically.

We overcome objections, we share, we communicate—we share in a transactional, personalized way with another person. So, too, the public speaker encodes and sends.

Message

The public speaker-sender produces a message as a product of the encoding and sending that takes place before and during speaking. The message is the tangible result of the encoding process communicated in a logical arrangement (sending) so that the listener-receiver can create, via receiving and decoding, a message very similar to the original thought, feeling or idea conveyed by the speaker.

The creation of a message is the process of changing the idea (feeling, attitude, etc.) into a set of words and/or nonwords arranged in an order that is clear and understandable. Complicated? Yes! We create content, however, every day in—yes, you guessed it—our conversations. We create a message in exactly the same way for a speech made in public. The major difference is that we "enlarge" the process. For instance, for public presentations we usually must do some research, possibly interview experts on our subject and we need to think through (encode) our own knowledge and experience. In addition, we must adjust our word choice and action for a public rather than private setting (higher intimacy). We also must develop a logical pattern to follow so our public communication has organization, definition and style (More about this in Chapter 6).

Noise

In the transactional model, noise refers to three kinds of interference, or distraction, which can block or distort communication. These three distractions are; external noise, semantic noise and internal noise.

External noise is defined as any interference outside the communication participants which distorts effective communication. The sounds of cross-talk (chatting between audience members during a public speech), music, interruptions such as late-comers, a too cold or hot room, poor acoustics, laughter, cigarette smoke and illness constitute some typical external sources of noise. An individual's accent may be the source of external noise if the sounds are not understandable to the listener. The speaker must adjust to his kind of noise or risk failure to communicate. The key word here is **adjust**. Either the noise must be eliminated or the speaker must adjust and correct for the condition(s). The audience, too, must adapt to the situation so as not to disrupt the speaker or other audience members by creating external noise. We do this naturally while in conversation. For example, we move away from the cigarette smoke or ask the smoker to stop. Or, if our thoughts are wandering we refocus by asking internal questions (e.g., "I wonder how I can use this information?") or questions of the speakers (e.g., "Could you repeat that? I'm distracted with this headache."). We can learn to adjust in similar ways when we are in a public speaking situation.

Internal noise refers to mental processes within either communication participant that interfere with effective communication. Have you ever caught yourself worrying about an important relationship while you were "listening" to a speech? Ever stop listening to someone because you dislike the sounds of a certain accent? Ever tune out a speaker because of a headache? Ever stop listening because you did not like the speaker? Ever have trouble understanding the speaker because you were distracted by what the speaker wore? These internal noise factors interfere with receiving and decoding a message. The speaker, too, can become distracted by internal noise in the form of thoughts such as, "I'm scared to death." "I 'm blushing." "What was I saying?" "They aren't listening." It is possible to become sensitive to facial expression, which is expressing negative internal noise, and adjust to it by asking questions directly to the audience. For example,

"Is that clear?" "Does this make sense?" "Is there something wrong?," and, if so, "Perhaps I can put this another way." If an audience is giving you signals of severe restlessness, a very legitimate response might be, "Let's take a 5-minute break and try again after we have all had a chance to relax and stretch our legs."

Semantic noise is that mental interference that comes from negative internal responses to certain words or the use of words. Poor grammar or mispronounced words cause semantic noise for some individuals. Certain words can block communication because of what they symbolize to the decoder. For example, words such as; pig, honey, gal, jock, stupid, communist, democrat, republican, snob. The public speaker needs to be aware of the importance of language and pronunciation as potential communication stoppers. When in conversation, we adapt when we see a friend blush or furrow her brow in response to something we say. We clarify, rephrase or apologize, if necessary. As public speakers we have the responsibility to try to avoid using verbal or nonverbal expression we know may offend. Further, as public speakers we need to be prepared to adjust and adapt if we inadvertently create semantic noise in our listeners—just as we would in our conversation. **CAUTION**—what creates semantic noise in one individual may or may not create semantic noise in another.

Delivery

There are four traditional methods, or modes, of presentation/delivery of a speech:

- ❑ Manuscript Speech: A speech written and delivered, word for word. This speech is prepared in order to be read.
- ❑ Memorized Speech: A speech memorized and delivered without notes.

- ❑ Extemporaneous Speech: A planned, prepared and practiced speech which allows the specific words, phrases and nonverbal communication to form themselves at the time of delivery. This delivery is idea centered.
- ❑ Impromptu Speech: A speech in which the speaker has little or no time to prepare.

All four modes of delivery have advantages and disadvantages. There is a time and place for each mode of speech delivery.

The manuscript speech is written and then read. The manuscript speech is useful when there is need for precision such as a technical, legal, political, medical or policy speech. The problems with this format have to do with the time and style of preparation as well as the amount of practice needed to sound and appear spontaneous in delivery. Most beginning public speakers are not trained to write for the ear nor are they yet polished interpreters of the written word. Because of this, many manuscript speeches sound stilted, artificial or awkward.

The memorized speech is written and then committed to memory, word for word. If the speaker is a gifted actor, this style can present a greater impact in delivery. Three primary problems exist with this approach. First, if the speaker is not a gifted actor, memorization can increase symptoms of speech fright, such as lapses in memory and the confusion this creates. Second, the memorized speech often sounds mechanical or unnatural. Third, and most important, the memorized speech does not allow for any audience or situation adaptation before or during the speech.

The impromptu speech is the type of delivery we use every day in conversations, meetings, interviews, and even family gatherings.

The impromptu delivery occurs when we speak spontaneously with little or no preparation. We rely on personal experience and logic to communicate. The effective impromptu speaker has the advantage of being able to communicate clearly and concisely on a moment's notice. The disadvantages of this approach have to do with poor conversational habits and lack of structure to guide us. Without the enlargements of planning, practice and organization we tend to ramble, offer incomplete thoughts and become nonfluent or repetitive. The key is to become aware of organizational structures on which to rely when circumstances call for impromptu speaking (see Chapter 12).

The extemporaneous speech is an enlarged conversation. It is planned but not memorized: Certain phrases or examples may be committed to memory but not the entire speech. It is informal, yet organized: It is open to adjustment. For example, the speaker-sender can skip a point, elaborate another, adjust the time of the event, and the speaker can respond easily to feedback from the audience. The advantage to the extemporaneous style is this—the speech is dynamic, idea centered and transactional. The disadvantage to the extemporaneous delivery is that it can never be exactly reproduced because it is the product of simultaneous invention and interpretation (encoding/decoding) by one audience and one speaker in one setting for their combined, unique shared experience. The fine extemporaneous speech combines the best of good conversational speaking, impromptu speaking and the elements of manuscript speaking. I prefer the extemporaneous delivery for most situations because it gives the speaker time to prepare and practice the overall structure and content yet allows the speaker to be fresh, conversational, flexible and alive.

Listener-Receiver (Participant)

When we play this role, we are engaged in a complex, simultaneous process of communication with the speaker-sender. We must hear and see the symbols produced by the speaker and then organize them into meaning for ourselves (decode). The meaning of the message is determined by the listener based on what we know about the speaker's topic and language. As listeners, we also decide on the degree of importance of the message. We bring our own experience, attitudes, needs and motives to the public speech and we make judgments as to whether the speech is interesting, challenging, boring, informative, repetitious, etc. Finally, we sum up the speech and attach our meaning of the message spoken by the sender.

It is the responsibility of the listener (audience) to aid in the communication event known as the public speech. It takes both the speaker and the audience to make the communication event happen. By your feedback as a listener, you guide the speaker (Remember, the effective public speaker is paying attention to the messages you send as you listen!). If you are appreciating the message, show it in your nonverbal communication. This will encourage the speaker who will be, in turn, more comfortable and will continue speaking effectively. The same holds true if you dislike the message or simply do not understand it. The point is this—if you are truthful in your comments, you will help the speaker. In short, both speaker and audience win.

Feedback

Feedback is the message you receive back from your listeners. It can be verbal or nonverbal. In the public speech context, most listener feedback is nonverbal but can take the form of verbal energy through questions, encouraging remarks or indicating the speaker has miscalculated. Feedback allows the speaker to know if he is heard, seen, understood, appreciated or believed.

The important thing about feedback is that it is the message the audience sends back to the speaker which allows her to adjust. By watching and listening to the listener's feedback the speaker adapts to the message sent to her by the audience ("keep talking," "give me an example," "so what?"). Each audience response is or can be used as corrective feedback for the next idea to be presented.

Setting/Situation/Context

Communication is influenced by the situation, or context, in which we speak. Consider how the following situations change the way we communicate:

- Conversation with a friend
- A funeral expressing sympathy
- A toast at a wedding
- Informing employees of a new policy
- Telling a child a story
- A public speech to motivate people to vote
- A class assignment
- A job interview
- A commencement address

Now consider how you would change your prepared remarks if the setting contained any or all of these elements:

- Over-crowded room
- Too hot
- Too cold
- Extreme noise (e.g., jets, trains, construction)
- Noisy/talkative audience
- Nonfunctioning microphone

The point is this—public speaking does not happen in a vacuum. The effective speaker must adapt his language to the situation and the people involved. If the context is formal, then formal language is acceptable. The more informal the situation, the more acceptable informal language. Does the audience understand slang? How "familiar" can you be with your audience? What is the mood of your speaking situation? How much does the audience already know about your topic? Can the audience easily see and hear? The answers to these questions tell the speaker how to approach speech preparation and delivery.

What is happening when we speak to others? That was my opening question in this chapter. You can now see that much is happening—that communication, whether interpersonal or public, is a complex process involving the speaker-sender, message, noise, delivery, listener-receiver, feedback and the situation/context. What is happening is that in public communication a speaker shares ideas with the listeners in a transaction that is really a series of one-to-one conversations. The transactional approach allows you to experience public speaking as a superb conversation that is known as — the enlarged conversation.

Remember; in the transactional process of communication all participants simultaneously send/speak and receive/listen. This is most evident in conversation. In public speaking the situation calls for a designated speaker who is, if effective, listening to the feedback being "spoken"/sent by the audience. Input from all participants effects the outcome of the communication event.

Diversity Issues Regarding the Communication Process

1. Think of five language examples that could be the source of semantic noise for audience members identifying with a culture other than your own. How might these effect the overall message?

2. Becoming aware of our distractions is the first step in managing them. As you listen to speakers from cultures other than your own -- what are some issues of noise, which interfere with your communication? What issues of noise might you perceive the speaker experiencing which are generated from your cultural identification? How does this effect your understanding of the overall message?

Critical Thinking Issues Regarding the Communication Process

1. What evidence can you collect and evaluate that will tell you whether you have been understood by your audience? How valid is this evidence?

2. As a member of the audience, how can you help the speaker communicate with you more clearly?

3. As a speaker, how can you help the audience better listen to you?

4. What are the pros and cons of each delivery mode? As an audience member, do you responding differently to each delivery mode?

Exercises: Applying the Chapter to Your Life

1.   To understand more fully the concept of the communication participant as simultaneous speaker and listener -- ask a friend to converse with you. While interacting, close your eyes or turn your back away from your friend so that you cannot receive any visual feedback.   How does this effect your overall understanding? What forms of noise are generated during this conversation?

2.   Choose three individuals with whom you converse on a regular basis. Choose someone with whom you are very familiar, someone who is your acquaintance, and an individual who you know in a very limited way. Plan to discuss some event that occurred to you over the past weekend. Discuss the same event with each of the three individuals, separately. How did your conversation with each person differ? How were they similar? Focus on --

     ❑ Depth of topic
     ❑ Formality/informality of language
     ❑ Emotional comfort
     ❑ Length of conversation
     ❑ Eye contact
     ❑ Gestures
     ❑ Setting

If all three individuals were in the same room at the same time and you were telling this small audience about that same event -- how would these categories, listed above, change? What does this tell you about message adaptation from one-on-one conversation to the public speaking situation?

Chapter 4:
Blending Theory, Art
& Skill - Public Speaking
Competence

W hat is communication competence? Why is it important for us to understand? In order to answer these questions we must look at two major views of communication/public speaking competence, why we communicate and the three major skill areas of public speaking.

Aristotle's View of Public Speaking Competence

Since about 450 B.C. (when the Greek instructors, Corax and Tisias, wrote a book on speech) there have been attempts to describe communication competence. Aristotle, in 336 B.C., described three aspects of public speaking competence which he believed have tremendous influence on the audience. He called these speaker competencies **logos**, **pathos**, and **ethos**. Aristotle's work left us with a systematic way to begin thinking about and improving our public speaking competency. His work suggests that speakers who rely on the three "proofs" (logos, pathos and ethos) will engage audience members to listen to, reason and feel with, and believe them.

According to Aristotle, logos is the word used to designate the speaker's use of reasoning, scientific method and expert opinion. Logos forms the content or substance of a speech and contains three elements: (1) claim or assertion, (2) objective support for the claim, and (3) a discussion to provide the logical link between the claim and the evidence.

Pathos was Aristotle's word for the emotional elements of the message. These elements are primarily the nonverbal aspects of communication. Elements of public speaking that represent pathos include the showing of any emotions; humor, fear, sorrow, excitement, etc. These feelings are shown through the use of voice, face, eyes, hands, the body and some elements of language (word choice).

Ethos, the third element of "proof," has to do with the speaker's believability, or credibility. No matter how brilliantly the speaker's message is invented and structured, the person speaking must be seen as sincere, competent and trustworthy in order to be believed. Nonverbal communication plays a very important part in the development of ethos (more later in this chapter).

As you continue your study of this chapter you will discover that, while modern communication researchers have come to understand so much about the communication and public speaking processes, we still carry over much of Aristotle's observations -- modern research simply has given greater depth and newer names to the three "proofs."

Modern View of Public Speaking Competence

Generally, a competent communicator is a person who, through an understanding of the principles of the communication process and knowledge of skills (behaviors), has the ability to communicate effectively. We can graphically represent communication competence as follows:

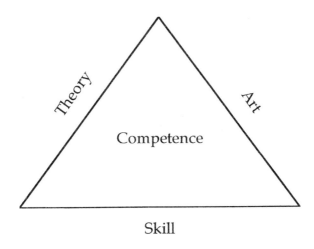

Skill

Alternatively, another way to depict a model of communication competence is:

Competence = Theory + Skill + Art

In the competence models, theory is defined as the principles of the discipline. Art refers to human style and human flexibility (choice and adaptability) in the communication process. Skill refers to the ability to act out certain behaviors that are known to be effective.

If speech instructors could teach you every skill you would ever need to know for any situation then communication competence would be a very simple achievement. Because communication is a process that is unique to time, place and individuals involved, we as communicators need to be inventive. We need to make educated decisions about what might or might not be appropriate behavior.

As the models suggest, we attempt our educated guesses via a three-step process: First, we come to understand the principles of how communication works and why we communicate (theory). Second, we come to understand ourselves as individuals with our particular styles of communicating (art). Third, we learn essential skills that have been known to be effective (although in human communication, nothing is completely predictable). There is a final step -- when we understand the communication process, our individual style and are able to behave in effective ways, we then can adapt in a multitude of situations. This is being a competent communicator.

Chapter 3 focused on the principles of the public speaking process -- how communication works in the public speaking context. Throughout your speech communication course, you will be developing an understanding of your own personal style. The remaining chapters of this text focus on the many speaking skills known to be effective. The remainder of this chapter focuses on why we communicate, why we communicate in the public speaking context and the three major skill areas of public speaking.

Why We Communicate

We communicate to fulfill needs. Just which needs we fulfill has been discussed at great length over the years. The scholars most often referenced in terms of communication needs are Abraham Maslow and William Schutz.

Abraham Maslow (1954) delineated a hierarchy of needs that we fulfill through communication. Briefly, Maslow stated that we have basic needs. These are: **physiological** (need for air, food, water), **safety** (freedom from harm), **social** (need to belong), **esteem** (need to excel as an individual), and **self-actualization** (complete personal fulfillment). The needs are arranged in a hierarchy so that until our physiological needs are fulfilled we cannot move to the next level, safety, and so on. If we are operating on a higher level, say esteem, and our safety is threatened, safety will then become our primary concern: this, then, becomes what we talk about or what motivates us to communicate. Maslow's hierarchy is discussed further in Chapter 13.

William Schutz (1966) describes three needs we all attempt to meet through communication; **Inclusion** (the need to belong), **control** (the need to be able to influence others) and **affection** (the need to care for and be cared for by others). The public speaker can meet any of these needs by sharing her ideas, dreams, information, humor, insight, enthusiasm, code of ethics, hopes, motivation and ability to persuade.

More on Schutz's need for control: Control refers to the lessening of uncertainty. We talk in order to reduce uncertainty. In the process of thinking through our speech topic, we begin to gain an understanding of a position, situation or problem. By organizing, then sharing what we are learning, we begin to discover order and predictability in our topic area. We thereby reduce uncertainty. We have a need to feel in control of our information, our selves and, to some extent, other people. The process of thinking through, organizing and sharing our communication allows us to gain this kind of control over uncertainty.

Why We Communicate in the Public Speaking Context

As communicators, we do communicate in order to fulfill the needs as expressed by Schutz and Maslow. This is true, also, in the public speaking context. We must consider further why we communicate in the public context regarding our purpose for speaking to the audience. There are four purposes, reasons, why we stand before an audience and communicate: to **promote change**, to **inform**, to **evoke**, and to **entertain**.

We Talk to Manage or Promote Change

When we are in the process of change, and that is an ongoing process, we talk to make sense of it. We communicate to help discover ways to understand or analyze the change. We talk to reduce our anxiety about change. We also talk to help others understand and deal with changes. For instance, the manager in an organization is often called on to explain a policy change. She may also attempt to persuade employees to change their behavior or alter an attitude. Some communication experts believe all communication contains elements of persuasion (See Chapter 13 for a complete discussion of persuasion and change through public speaking.).

We Talk to Share Information

This is called the speech to inform (See Chapter 11 for a detailed discussion about this type of speech.). Sometimes we share information about ourselves, such as in a job interview, or we share what we know about a given topic during a formal test or in a discussion situation. Or, perhaps we talk through and explain a procedure, idea or process. We may provide information that keeps the listener current with the news of the day. We often talk to create a shared understanding of our world.

We Talk to Evoke an Emotion

Sometimes the reason driving us to speak is that we want the audience to respond on an emotional level. The eulogy is an example of an evocative speech. Speaking to inspire is also a speech to evoke. For instance, a coach at halftime may speak in order to evoke enthusiasm and pride from his team players. The speech to entertain is a specific form of a speech to evoke.

The speaker with a sense of humor uses wit, humor or personal stories to offer the listener a break from the stresses of the day. The speech to entertain is given to help the audience feel good -- to have a good time. The speaker who uses humor lightens our mood.

Three Major Skill Areas of Public Speaking

As stated earlier in this chapter, public speaking competence is the combination of theory, art and skill. We have discussed that part of communication theory dealing with why we communicate -- the remaining chapters of this text continue to focus on specific aspects of public speaking theory. Your work in this course will develop your artistic style as a speaker. Throughout this text, skills are delineated to help you develop as a public speaker. While these skills are varied and many, they fall into three major areas of focus: **organization, appropriate content and language,** and **appropriate nonverbal communication.**

Organization

The public speaker is required to be organized. As listeners we expect and need a pattern when we listen to a speech. When the speaker moves along from beginning to end in one consistent direction, we say that the speech is organized. Chapter 6 is dedicated entirely to speech organization.

Appropriate Content

The language of a speech reflects the content of a speech. Specifically, the content is based on the words we choose, the verbal communication we share. We choose appropriate language and use it as evidence, or support, for our ideas. Aristotle referred to this as logos. What language we choose and how we organize it depends on the type of speech and audience. Chapters 10 through 13 specifically address the various public speaking contexts and their individual demands on language.

Appropriate Nonverbal Communication

In face-to-face communication, the speaker communicates more nonverbally than with words. Public speaking is face-to-face communication.

The research of Birdwhistell (1970) and others has shown that about 65% of our total message is communicated by what we do rather than what we say. Mehrabian's (1971) research indicates that over 90% of the emotional impact of our communication is nonverbal: 55% of the message is communicated by the face, 38% of the message is communicated by the voice and only 7% of the message is conveyed by words alone.

Nonverbal communication can be defined as communication without words. The following types of nonverbal behavior are most often cited in research and are very important to the public speaker.

- ❑ **Facial Communication**: How our facial movements create or reinforce meanings; the smile, frown, tight lips, biting the lip, etc.
- ❑ **Body Communication**: How gesture, movement, energy and body type communicate meaning to an audience; wringing of hands, free flowing gestures, low/high energy, tall and thin body, short and fat body, rocking back and forth, etc.
- ❑ **Eye Communication**: How we use eye contact, in terms of length of contact or avoidance of contact, to communicate. When we make eye contact, we are saying, "I have you in my sight -- I want to talk with you." We engage our audience by making eye contact.

- **Vocal Communication**: The use of pitch, voice quality, rate, loudness and softness to communicate shades of meaning or feeling.
- **Artificial Communication**: How hairstyle, make-up, clothing, jewelry and color communicate our personality as part of our message. While there is some correlation between artificial communication and personality, research indicates that it is not entirely predictable -- yet we think we know people by their looks. Have you ever been surprised to find out that the person you were with was not as they dressed? Remember that your audience, too, will probably think they know you by the way you look.

Nonverbal communication is something we do at all times -- we cannot turn nonverbal communication on and off. Even if you are sitting in a chair, doing "nothing," your nonverbal communication is telling others that you are sitting in a chair, doing "nothing." This is what is meant by, *you cannot not communicate.*

Researchers have identified several types and functions of nonverbal communication:

- To accent or emphasize our words.
- To complement or reinforce our words.
- To regulate or control the flow of words.
- To contradict or send a message that is directly opposite the verbal meaning (e.g., sarcasm).
- To substitute or take the place of words.

Our nonverbal behavior can communicate either intentionally or unintentionally. Our words may say we are glad to be speaking with a particular audience but our face can reflect the opposite feeling. Our voice may also betray our true feelings although our words contradict those feelings. As a rule, when nonverbal communication contradicts the verbal, we believe the nonverbal message. Effective speakers communicate a consistent message, using the verbal and nonverbal aspects as desired.

Our society and our broader culture tell us what is appropriate and inappropriate in nonverbal communication. For example, we can yell at a football game but not during a speech. In addition, we need to make eye contact with our audience while speaking but not stare too long at any one person.

Nonverbal behaviors are best understood as a collection of signals. When we communicate that we are pleased to be the public speaker for an occasion we do so by our eye contact, facial expression, posture, energy level, voice, even our choice of dress. The words we speak may be immaterial if our nonverbal "package" contradicts the words we use. When there are differences between what is said ("I'm pleased to be here") and what is done (no eye contact), we notice the differences and begin to focus on and believe nonverbal signals.

For the public speaker, a cluster of dysfunctional (usually unintentional) nonverbal behaviors can destroy the speaker's intended message. The following nonverbal behaviors are considered dysfunctional:

- ❑ Any behavior that interferes with the speaker's intended message.
- ❑ Any behavior which causes either the sender or receiver to feel emotionally uncomfortable.
- ❑ Any behavior that creates a relationship problem between the sender and receiver.
- ❑ Any behavior which communicates a negative impression of an individual or group in the audience or elsewhere.
- ❑ Contradictory nonverbal behaviors which interfere with the overall positive tone of the speaking situation, including the speaker.

Words help us express our ideas; indeed, they form our specific ideas. Our voice, face, eyes, dress, posture, gestures and appearance express our feelings and attitudes. In public speech we need both head (verbal content) and heart (nonverbal behaviors) functioning together in order to communicate skillfully and artfully.

Techniques to Improve
Your Nonverbal Communication

- Read aloud as often as possible to improve voice, diction, volume and ability to phrase smoothly.
- Audiotape record yourself when you are practicing a speech. Evaluate how you organize, how you use pitch, how you use silence and vocal variety to make your points.
- Videotape can be very useful. Have a friend record you in a variety of situations such as conversing with a friend, walking, dancing, rehearing a speech, reading material from the newspaper or presenting an oral report in class. Review the tapes with your friend. What nonverbal behavior do you need to change in order to communicate better your message?

Further Points to Consider Regarding
Nonverbal Communication

- We cannot not communicate. Everything we do or do not do "says" something.
- Communication is self-reflective. We communicate something about ourselves no matter our content or organization. Our nonverbal communication is always busy "telling" others who we are, our attitudes, likes and dislikes and more.

- First impressions form very quickly and are resistant to change. These impressions are primarily formed from nonverbal cues and guide the receiver to judge or interpret the speaker's behavior or motives.
- Each person has unique nonverbal behavior. We need to avoid stereotyping a speaker's nonverbal signals. Avoiding eye contact or dressing a certain way may mean different things to different people. What we think a speaker's behavior means may be wrong. We need to look for patterns and consistencies or inconsistencies before we make our judgements.
- Finally, I remind you that at least 65% of your message is communicated by nonverbal behavior. You become a more skilled speaker as you become aware of your own nonverbal behaviors.

Public speaking competence is acquired through an understanding of pertinent communication theory, development of specific skills and through understanding and developing your own "artful" communication style. You can learn what it takes to be a competent public speaker. Becoming competent takes time, practice and the willingness to look at how you communicate now and enhance what works and replace those ineffective behaviors.

Diversity Issues Regarding Communication Competence

1. What importance does your culture place on communicating to promote change? Share information? Entertain? Evoke an emotion? Discuss this question with someone from outside of your culture. Share your answers with one another. What did you learn?
2. Research the differences and similarities of facial expressions within different cultures. While we all may view the same face -- our culture tells us how to interpret the expression. The same

expression may be interpreted differently by different cultures. This is true of all nonverbal communication.

3. As a class, discuss what is considered appropriate content by the various cultures represented in your class.

Critical Thinking Issues Regarding Communication Competence

1. Typically, the greater United States culture uses inductive reasoning, the greater European culture uses deductive reasoning, while the greater Asian culture uses intuitive (the reasoning process is not so much concerned with logic and analysis as it is with intuition and meditative introspection -- nonAristotelian). (Klopf, pg. 117) How might these differences affect us as both speaker and listener in understanding messages from a critical thinking standpoint?

2. How do we know if our message content is appropriate before ever presenting our speech to the audience?

3. What are some of the ethical issues facing the public speaker regarding the presentation of certain material to an audience being driven by Maslow's safety need? Social need? Physiological need? Any of the five needs?

4. Discuss the validity of this premise: The modern view of public speaking competence is, in fact, a view of critical thinking.

Exercises: Applying the Chapter to Your Life

1. Keep a journal of how you interact nonverbally with one of your friends in different contexts over time. Focus on:

   ❑ One-on-one private interaction context (e.g., alone at home)
   ❑ One-on-one public interaction context (e.g., eating in a restaurant)
   ❑ With other friends in private (e.g., at someone's home or riding in a car)
   ❑ With other friends in public (e.g., on the college campus or in the lobby of a theater)

   Note changes in as many nonverbal behaviors as possible. What do these discoveries tell you about the similarities and differences in appropriate nonverbal behavior in the informal conversation as opposed to the more formal public setting?

2. Think of as many topics as you can that you personally enjoy discussing with a friend but would be uncomfortable discussing in front of a room full of acquaintances or strangers. What does this tell you about the appropriateness of topic in the public speaking context?

3. Observe someone you believe to be well organized in his communication. What does he do to encourage you to follow along with very little effort on your part? Is it his choice of topic? Amount of information shared? What?

   Now, observe another individual whom you find disorganized and difficult to understand. Compare this person's communication behavior with those behaviors of the well-organized communicator.

Using Humor in Your Speech

Humor. Is laughter really the best medicine? I think so. So did Norma Cousins who wrote the best selling book, *Anatomy of an Illness as perceived by the Patient.* Cousins wrote his book to document how he used humor (humor therapy) to help cure himself from a terminal disease.

Cousins was also a very effective public speaker who used humor to help carry his message to his huge audiences. He used humor to unify his listeners and to win their support as well as to make them feel good.

We associate humor, particularly here in America, with wit, intelligence and command of the situation. We seem to be saying, "If a person can make us laugh he/she is really cool, calm and in control."

Humor, that unique human characteristic, can ease tension in stressful situations when nothing else will lift our spirits. I was recently reminded of how healing, unifying and powerful humor can be by the eulogy presented at a memorial service for a young colleague of mine who died from cancer. The speaker was the first of several speakers. He chose to highlight his boyhood recollections of his deceased friend, Fred (name changed for privacy). He deliberately used humorous stories about himself and Fred. In moments, a very somber group of mourning people was uplifted. We laughed and marveled at the human comedy being shared by a man who obviously loved and knew his friend. We learned how to celebrate his life. Even on such a painful occasion as this, humor healed. Humor saved the day.

Humor, wit, and personal stories can allow the public speaker to keep the interest of an audience, gain and regain attention when they drift away from the speech content. Politicians, teachers, clergy and others use humor (even judges use humor) to ease tension, or to avoid pomposity. A well timed self "put down" can form an instant favorable connection between speaker and audience. A shared laugh can break the artificial barrier often built between speaker and listener. Humor is an instrument of goodwill -- a human connection.

I am quite certain you have heard speeches that were organized, important, sometimes interesting but mostly dull. The problem can be a lack of joy or a lack of a sense of playfulness from the speaker.

However, do we have to become comedians in order to hold an audience? NO! We do not expect a serious speaker addressing a serious subject to have all the comic skills of a Bill Cosby or Jay Leno. Nevertheless, today's audiences do expect the serious speaker to use wit and to feel free enough to share a humorous story (anecdote) or perhaps reveal a humorous personal shortcoming in order to relate better. The audience often sees the speaker as more "human" when she can laugh at herself. The audience also seems to enjoy it when the speaker can "lighten" a serious topic, thus giving another perspective, as well as relieving some tension.

But how can we do this? There are some specific principles to introduce humor and wit into our presentations. We do not have to present an entertaining monologue. We can use humor in most any speech. We can work it into the content of the speech. Humor is an adjunct, or aid, to the serious speaker who wishes to lighten and highlight a presentation. Here are some techniques that are proven to produce humorous results:

Use exaggeration. The use of an outlandish hyperbole (exaggeration) can introduce wit and humor into your speech. Be sure to make it clear that you are grossly overstating so no one takes your comment literally. A student speaker caught me by surprise when he said, "Most people listen four times as fast as the average person can speak. My girlfriend has that all wrong -- she speaks four times faster than I can listen!" Once he had our attention (and our laughter) he clarified by stating, "And I must tell you, in reality she is a terrific listener and speaker. I was just teasing."

Try an incongruous list. Make a list of essential ingredients or perhaps list the main points to be covered in your presentation. Then, slip in a ridiculous item. For example, one speaker listed her typical reactions to her first hot air balloon ride. She said, "Most of us shared the same feelings as we waited to step into the gondola -- that fragile wicker basket -- excitement, anticipation, awe and **sheer terror.**" A job applicant added this example list: "I should get this job because of my talent, temperament, training and because my car was just repossessed."

The anticlimax can be useful. The secret of the anticlimax is movement from serious to a dramatic collapse.

Mark Twain gave us this example: "Man is the only animal who blushes -- or needs to."

A humorous definition can maintain interest. You can create your own humorous definitions or you can find usable quotations in any library in such works as *Bartletts Familiar Quotations*. Here are a couple of examples:

❑ "Americans are endowed with life, liberty and the pursuit of their share of the national debt." (author unknown)
❑ "Most people's idea of a good sermon is one that goes over their head and hits their neighbor." (author unknown)

You may want to try the out-of-place comment to create surprise and generate a smile: "I don't want to get rich quickly. I just want to inherit a fortune — or marry one." Another example, the young couple was staring at a low flying airplane when he remarked, "That's a mail plane." She said, "How can you tell from this distance?"

You can learn to be funny. Look for ways to use these techniques in your daily conversations. You do not have to tell jokes but you can remember humorous personal stories that can help you relate refreshingly with your audience while spicing your content. You can learn to use the devices just discussed in most any public speech. But remember, the kind of humor we are suggesting you use is based on wit and should be thought of as the "spice" in your presentation — not the "main course" of your communication.

Chapter 5: The Role of the Audience

Chapters 2, 3, and 4 focused primarily on the role of the speaker/sender in the public communication setting. As you now know, communication is a continual, two-way process necessitating both speaker/sender and listener/receiver. This chapter focuses on the role of the audience, specifically, the role of the audience in the public speaking classroom.

The role of **audience** is familiar to everyone, but perhaps not in the sense of being a vital link in the creative communication process. The audience is appreciator, encourager, critic and enthusiast. The communicator must first conceptualize the idea, then bring it to life as speaker but it is the **audience** showing its need for or appreciation of the entire speech that keeps it all alive. For example, as the audience we need to show appreciation for what we like and offer critique of what disturbs. I believe, therefore, that a major part of courses in public speaking should include information regarding learning to be an effective audience member. In order to be fully functional as a class, I believe we must first become responsible: Being **here** is our primary responsibility to each other. It is not just being here, however, but *how* we are here that matters. **Our ultimate purpose is to find ways to increase our effectiveness.** As audience members and as speakers we need to sharpen our skills. Throughout the course, we will listen to fellow students and we will critique each other's attempts to speak effectively. We need to become skillful at listening and critiquing. *To be sure, you will be the featured speaker several times during* *the course but it is as audience that you have primary responsibilities during every meeting.*

The concept of **rhetorical sensitivity** is also an important goal for our overall classroom behavior. **Communicator styles** and **types of messages** will be examined and, finally, I will show how we might apply what we know of speech communication principles by emphasizing **dialogue** in our class.

Being Present

What do I mean by saying our first responsibility in this class is being present (being here)? Well, we obviously cannot communicate our thoughts, ideas, knowledge and feelings to each other if we are unable to interact. Simple. You are the audience. You have to be here!

At this point I submit a definition of communication between two people as, *a process of exchanging verbal and nonverbal messages in order to understand, influence, learn from, and relate to the other."* Put another way: we co-create understanding, learn from each other, change each other or simply feel uplifted as we communicate one with the other. This definition helps us see how we simultaneously interact as audience and how this interaction is effected by our commitment to listening, and, by the speaker's understanding of who she is talking with, and finally, by the relationship and level of trust that exits between the audience and speaker. **Put simply: We cannot relate, learn, influence or be influenced, help, or understand unless we are present and aware of each other!**

Being present is first, right? Nothing much can be communicated if we are not present to hear, see, understand, and relate to each other. But it is possible to be present physically and not present psychologically. For example, how often do you fail to listen to another person? How often do you mentally debate the speaker rather than listen? How often do you make an early judgment about the speaker or the message and fail to hear what is really being said? How often do you indulge in a premature negative emotional response to a speaker or the subject and thereby short-circuit your ability to respond rationally to the message? How often do you tune out early as listener because you feel forced, stressed or uninterested? If we can answer that we have fallen, indeed, to these normal distractions, we are guilty of nonlistening behaviors and we need to consider how to improve our communicative effectiveness.

Competencies

We had to learn whatever competence we have as communicators. Excellent speakers/listeners have learned the rules for effective interaction and can perform the rules well in most situations although they may not be conscious of the rules they are following. Communication researcher Spitzberg (1988) reports **competent speakers** do the following:

- Speak fluently
- Know when to take turns talking
- Look at the other when talking
- Show understanding or approval by being active listeners -- nodding head saying, "um-hmm," etc.
- Compliment the other person often
- Smile and laugh occasionally and appropriately
- Use gestures when speaking

James Floyd's research (1993) suggests the following **listening behaviors** as rules for effective listening (and for our classroom, too):

- Stop talking!
- Listen for ideas (listen for the message not the messenger)
- Ask questions
- Listen (and stay tuned) for unexpected information
- Do not argue until you really know what the speaker means
- Avoid distractions -- if a thought comes to mind, write it down, then listen. Do whatever you can to avoid distractions in the setting -- move, if necessary, or ask others to be quiet.

Most important, for our classroom situation, I expect you to become other-oriented. This means:

- Being aware of who your audience is when speaking to us.
- Listening without distracting the speaker or other audience members.
- Being on time so a speaker is not interrupted by your late entry.
- Providing thoughtful feedback when in critique sessions with fellow students
- Staying focused on the messages being presented and on the speaker's style and thought, not on yourself
- Putting aside your personal life for approximately three hours a week so that you can fully invest your unique brand of attention
- Supporting your peers in the most positive way possible

Rhetorical Sensitivity

In addition to becoming competent public speakers and audience members, my most hoped-for outcome for this course is that you become **rhetorically sensitive**. Two communication researchers, R.

Hart and D. Burks (1987) developed the original formulation for a special communication effectiveness we call, rhetorical sensitivity.

According to Hart and Burks, the rhetorically sensitive person has concern for self and others. The rhetorically sensitive show six characteristics:

First, the person is aware that we are, in fact, many different selves -- not a single self. We change our communication behaviors from situation (or context) to situation. Hart and Burk indicate that we need to learn (or "be trained," in their words) to select the roles which are appropriate to time, place, situation and person(s) involved. For instance, interrupting, cross-talking or belittling are not appropriate communication behaviors or roles during a classmate's speech. While some of these roles or behaviors might be appropriate in some other narrow contexts, they certainly would not be acceptable in the example given of the public speech classroom.

Second, the rhetorically sensitive person does not communicate in the same way in all situations. This communicator will avoid stylized, inflexible communication which never varies but is able to adapt behaviors to fit the occasion, time, audience, etc.

Third, the rhetorically sensitive person will adapt behavior on the basis of a given communication (i.e., be able to change thoughts, modify beliefs, or attitudes and behavior. The RS (rhetorically sensitive) person will consider making changes in thought or belief before breaking off and interaction. In other words, this person will hear the other person out, ask questions and be willing to adapt a new position without being defensive. (Can you do this? Sometimes I still have difficulty doing this when faced with data that forces me to change my self-perception or change a belief or attitude.)

Fourth, the RS person does not engage in self-fulfilling prophecy. This is done when we predict without adequate information that no behavior we could change or adapt would make any difference -- have any effect on self or other involved in the communication.

Fifth, the RS person is aware that feelings of anger or disagreement may not be appropriate to communicate in all situations -- that in some situations this is not acceptable behavior. Sometimes the only RS thing to do is say nothing. Also, the RS person does not overload the listener(s) with irrelevant, abstract detail to make an impression. Instead, the RS person is concerned with providing needed data and no more. Total candor can also be destructive. We are not being RS if we dump whatever is on our minds on the other person(s) without regard for either the need for or possible impact of such candor.

Sixth, the RS person understands ideas can be expressed in many different ways. When feelings are running high (when we are expressing our frustration or anger, for instance) there are productive ways to ventilate these feelings without attacking the other person.

The formulation of RS behavior was a reaction to self-disclosive behavior that took no heed of the impact of the communication behavior on the listener. Current researchers have supported Hart and Burk's research and conclusions. For example, in 1996, S. Littlejohn said, *[we can see] ... effective communication does not arise from blatant openness and disclosure but from sensitivity and care in adjusting what you say to your listener.*

Dialogue

So, what can we do to create the most effective communication climate for our speech communication classroom? In a word, we might strive for what I will call **dialogue**. Dialogue, as a way of communicating, puts a premium on listening and is aimed toward trying to understand others' points of view. It is being constructive and responsible when offering suggestions for improvement. Dialogue maximizes cooperation and keeps the communicator focused on issues, ideas, character, values and principles. Dialogue is a way of helping us delay our emotional responses until the other person has completed her message. Dialogue, as our primary approach to this class, allows us to give the other person his or her time to speak. Those in dialogue seek the truth not the destruction of the other person's character. The following guidelines translate abstract advice into behaviors that you can use to create confirming dialogue in our classroom:

❑ Acknowledge the Other Person. Acknowledging is not as obvious as it might seem. Pseudo-listening is as disconfirming as it is common. We often appear outwardly to be listening but our thoughts are elsewhere. We end up not knowing the message and running the risk of offending the speaker. A wandering glance, vacant expression, and inattentive posture all suggest you are not paying attention. If you interrupt, give irrelevant, tangential, ambiguous, or incongruous responses, these behaviors imply a disconfirming "I don't care about you" attitude. A complete acknowledgement combines two elements. The first is understanding of the speaker's *ideas*. We can confirm another's position by asking intelligent questions. An even clearer way to show you understand is to paraphrase the message. Messages like these do not agree or disagree with the sender. Rather, they show that you understand what the other person is saying. Conveying this sort of understanding might seem trivial until you realize how often others fail to acknowledge your ideas, and how frustrated this lack of acknowledgment leaves you. A second, more thorough kind of acknowledgement conveys your understanding of the speaker's *feelings*, as well as thoughts or ideas. The best way to show your understanding is by reflecting. Examples:

- "You really feel confident that your plan for changing the tuition at Central State will work, huh? It sounds like you are excited about giving it a try."
- "I never realized it before, but it sounds like you resent the way I tease you about your accent. You think I am putting you down, and that is what triggers your anger. Is that right?"

It helps to realize that acknowledging a message is not the same thing as agreeing with it.

- Demonstrate an Open-Minded Attitude. Ask questions, by all means, but make sure they are sincere requests for information, and not leading the speaker into a verbal trap.
- Agree Whenever Possible. Emphasizing shared beliefs makes it easier to discuss disagreements. A moment of thought will show that you probably share many important beliefs with others -- even those positions you dislike. Recognizing such shared beliefs will not resolve disagreements but can create a climate that makes discussion possible and productive.
- Describe, Do Not Evaluate. Statements that judge another person are likely to provoke a defensive reaction. **Evaluative language** has been described as **"you" language**, since most evaluative language contains an accusatory use of that word. For example:

  - "You made a fool of yourself in that speech."
  - "You smoke too much."
  - "You are not doing your share of the work in our speech group."

In contrast to this sort of evaluative language is **descriptive language**, often characterized as "I" language. Rather than judging another's behaviors, a descriptive statement explains the personal effect of the other's action. These descriptive statements are also known as

assertions. For example, instead of saying, "You talk too much," a descriptive communicator might say, "When you do not give me a chance to say what is on my mind, I get frustrated." This sort of descriptive statement contains three elements: (1) an account of the other person's behavior; (2) an explanation of how that behavior effects you, and (3) a description of the speaker's feelings about the communication behavior. Further examples:

- ❏ "When you told those jokes in your speech I got the impression that everyone seemed uncomfortable. I was really embarrassed."
- ❏ "When you take a break every 10 or 15 minutes, I wind up doing most of the work. I do not mind that once in a while, but I am getting fed up."

Defensiveness is likely to occur when one person attempts to impose an idea on others with little regard for their needs or interests. This sort of controlling communication is not only disconfirming -- it is often unnecessary. A more productive attitude is a problem-solving orientation: Asking, "How can we solve this problem?" instead of, "How can I '*smash*' the other person?"

- ❏ Communicate Honestly. Dishonesty and manipulation are destructive. Paradoxical as it seems, candor, too, can be a kind of manipulation. Some people use honesty in a calculating way, revealing just enough information to get what they want. When discovered, such candor can backfire, for it leaves the victim feeling like a sucker. Honesty *used as a weapon* can destroy a relationship more quickly than almost any other type of communication. Remember, the speaker and the audience are in a relationship. Further, the honest message needs to be delivered at the right time and in a way that is easy for the other person to understand. "You look terrible in that outfit" may be your honest feeling but it is not confirming. "I think

59

it is great that you are trying to change your look, but I would like you better in another outfit for your speeches" does confirm the speaker while still expressing your honesty.

Messages Are Best When Direct

The first requirement for effective self-expression is knowing when something needs to be said. This means that you do not assume people know what you think or want. This is best accomplished by being **clear**.

Messages Are Best When Clear

Here are some tips for staying clear:

- ❑ Do not ask questions when you need to make a statement.
- ❑ Keep your messages congruent. Your content, your tone of voice, and your body language should all fit together.
- ❑ Avoid double messages. Double messages are like kicking your dog and petting him at the same time. One message undercuts the other. For example, "I really like your speech but you are all wrong on your main point."
- ❑ Be clear about your wants and feelings.

    - ❑ Distinguish between observations and thoughts. You have to separate what you see and hear from your judgements, theories, beliefs and opinions.
    - ❑ Focus on one thing at a time.

Messages Are Best When Straight

A straight message is one in which the stated purpose is identical with the real purpose of the communication. Disguised intentions and hidden agendas destroy intimacy because they put you in a position of manipulating rather than relating to people. Being straight also means that you tell the truth.

Messages Are Clear When Supportive

Being supportive means that you want the other person to be able to hear you without becoming defensive. Ask yourself, "Do I want my message to be heard defensively or accurately? Is my purpose to hurt someone, to aggrandize myself, or to communicate?" Asking these questions makes you rhetorically sensitive. These following tactics do just the opposite -- thereby hurting your listener with your messages:

- ❑ **Global labels.** "Stupid," "ugly," "selfish," "evil," "mean," disgusting," "worthless," and "boring" are a few of the large list of hurtful words.
- ❑ **Sarcasm.** This form of humor very clearly tells the listener that you have contempt for him. It is often a cover for feelings of anger and hurt.
- ❑ **Negative comparisons.** "Why don't you try speaking like George?" Comparisons are deadly because they not only contain "you are bad" messages, but they trigger feelings of inferiority in others.
- ❑ **Judgmental "you" messages.** These attacks use an accusing form. "You do not deserve an 'A'. You bore me." This statement is pure judgement without any constructive focus on behavior.

Honest communication produces understanding and closeness while "win/lose" games produce warfare and distance. If you find yourself feeling defensive and wanting to criticize the other person, that is a clue that you are playing "win/lose."

The Four Kinds of Expression

Your communication with other people can be placed into four categories: expressing your **observations, thoughts, feelings**, and **needs**. Each category requires a different style of expression and, often, a very different vocabulary.

Observations

Observation means to report what your senses tell you. There are no speculations, inferences, or conclusions. Everything is simple fact. These are statements of observation:

- ❑ "I read in the *Sentinel* that an ice age is due to start within five hundred years."
- ❑ "My old address was 1996 Fell Street."
- ❑ "I broke the toaster this morning."

Feelings

Probably the most difficult part of communication is expressing our feelings. Some people do not want to hear what you feel. Anger is the most difficult feeling to receive because it can be threatening to the listener's self-esteem. Yet, how you feel is a large part of what makes you unique and special. Shared feelings are the building blocks of intimacy. When others are allowed to know what hurts, angers, frightens or pleases you, two things happen: These others have greater empathy and understanding and are better able to modify their behavior to meet your needs. Remembering to be rhetorically sensitive to the situation, you can share feelings and stimulate communication that is more productive.

Needs

No one knows what you need, except you. You are the expert, the highest authority on yourself. Needs are not judgmental. They do not blame or assign fault. They are simple statements about what would help or please you -- what you need! Examples:

- ❑ "I enjoy being with you. I also need my privacy."
- ❑ "I was a bit embarrassed by your off-color humor in the speech. In order to listen, I need to feel comfortable."
- ❑ "When you clearly organize your thoughts I can follow your ideas with ease and that triggers my excitement and I want to listen to you even more."

Whole Messages

Whole messages include all four kinds of expressions: what you see, think, feel, and need. It means giving accurate feedback about what you observe, clearly stating your inferences and conclusions, saying what emotions are triggered, and, if you need something, making straightforward requests or suggestions. Partial messages create confusion. People sense something is missing, but they do not know what. They may turn away from listening when they hear judgments untempered by your feelings and hopes. They may resist hearing anger that does not include the story of your frustration or hurt. These listeners may become suspicious of conclusions without supporting facts and observations. They may be uncomfortable with demands growing from unexpressed feelings and assumptions.

You can test whether you are giving whole or partial messages by asking the following questions:

- ❑ Have I expressed what I actually know to be fact? Is it based on what I have observed, read, or heard from reliable sources?
- ❑ Have I expressed and clearly labeled my inferences and conclusions?
- ❑ Have I expressed my objections without blame or judgment?
- ❑ Have I shared my ideas without judging the speaker's character?

Know Your Own Mind

Consider your own views. What do you think? Think through your beliefs before you speak. Be prepared to contribute every class meeting.

Knowing your own mind puts you miles ahead of many people who show up at class empty-headed, unprepared -- bored.

I started this chapter by saying how important it is to be effective, responsible audience members. If you can see how important it is to be **in dialogue** with each other, you will learn and grow in ways we cannot now even imagine. I believe you will become a better speaker in this class. Now, I am challenging you to commit fully to this learning experience by becoming more sensitive and effective as an audience member.

I cannot speak for you but I, personally, can tell when I am with a person or group reflecting a closed mind. I feel cramped and shut off to my possibilities. In the presence of people who say, in effect, "go for it," I feel an acceptance. I appreciate the absence of pre-judgement and I try to do my best.

There is another way you can help each other grow. Challenge! Encourage each other to try new speech projects. If, for example, I tell you I am afraid of something new because I do not think I have the ability to succeed and you encourage me and support me when the going gets tough, I might stick to the project. If I do, it has been my experience that I discover power and energy I never dreamed I had. You will have helped me transcend my incomplete self-concept by challenging and supporting me. I believe many of your classmates would respond in the same way as I would.

By being there, listening, empathizing, challenging, and offering rhetorically sensitive feedback, you support the work of the entire class. I invite you into dialogue!

Diversity Issues Regarding the Role of the Audience

1. What do you believe to be the expected and appropriate classroom behaviors of the student audience? Does this agree with the expectations presented in this chapter? With other classmates? With your professor?
2. Discuss the premise: The college classroom is a culture. Assuming this is a valid premise -- what are the implications of the responsibilities of the members of the culture regarding all behaviors, including communication behaviors? If you believe the premise to be invalid -- explain why.

Critical Thinking Issues Regarding the Role of the Audience

1. What are the ethical and moral issues facing the audience in the public speaking classroom?
2. How do these issues (from question #1) transfer to the audience outside the classroom?

Exercises: Applying the Chapter to Your Life

1. Observe each of the classrooms in which you spend time. What are the similar and different behavior expectations in each?
2. Observe how appropriate behavior is rewarded. What are the rewards? Who provides these rewards? Are the answers to these questions the same from classroom to classroom? Explain.
3. Observe how inappropriate audience behavior is negatively sanctioned (a mechanism of social control for enforcing a culture's standards). What are those sanctions? Who provides these sanctions? Who is/are the recipients of these sanctions? Are the answers to these questions the same from classroom to classroom? Explain.

Chapter 6: Planning the Route - Speaker as Tourguide

The most common reason for a speech to fail is lack of preparation during the process of composing the speech. I believe this is often the result of lack of direction. Many beginning speakers do not have a format to follow when they begin composing their speech. Questions such as,

"Where do I start?"
"What do I do first, second, third?"
"How do I proceed to a final product?"

plague us unless we have some sort of map to follow. I suggest you consider the following approach:

The Tourguide Metaphor

Consider using the metaphor of the "tourguide" as your map and compass in developing your speech organization. As a speaker, it is your task to take us, your audience, on a "tour" of your topic. We are ready to be guided along a "mind trip." You have the responsibility to be prepared to introduce the "tour," lead us through from one to five main ideas, relate to our needs, keep us interested and motivate us to participate actively in the "idea tour." You provide the structure -- we follow, appreciate and understand.

Here is an example of the beginning of such an "idea tour" on the topic of alcoholism:

Sample Introduction

"We are about to embark on a journey of understanding -- a journey to better understand alcoholism. How many of you believe you understand this word -- alcoholism? How many of you have taken a close look at all the essential elements of alcoholism? Well, for several reasons I've researched this topic. I'm delighted you're with me today because I have for you a unique view of the subject. I guarantee you will not see alcoholism in the same way after our time together. Our route takes us to see the social aspects of alcoholism. Then we move on to the biological aspects and, finally, we will explore the effects of this disease called alcoholism. Let's move on to our first stop: The social aspect of alcoholism..."

This "tourguide" metaphor is an extended metaphor and, by its nature, is simplified. But its principles are clear. By using this approach, the introduction establishes rapport with the audience (e.g., sense of speaker being there for the audience, "We are about to embark," "I'm delighted you're with me."), motivates them to want to know more ("a most unique view of the subject," "will not see alcoholism the same way."), provides an overview and scope of the main ideas to be covered in the speech (social, biological and effects of the disease). It provides structure for the speaker and the audience. As the speaker/tourguide leads the audience through each main point he says all that is necessary for comprehension of the major points of interest (main points) then moves on until the end of the tour, the conclusion, is reached. The conclusion, in this case, will recap the "tour," re-establish key concepts and provide a "clincher" (See Chapter 8 for more detail) which is challenging and easy to remember.

Why does this work? As listeners to a public speaker, we demand structure and are conditioned, in fact, to certain kinds of order. When we are given structure that makes sense to us we follow along easier and stay focused longer.

Common Organization Patterns
for Public Speaking

You already know the kinds of order that make sense to you. But here are some examples so you can identify the patterns you find most natural. You decide which pattern best serves your own speech composition needs:

- Cause-Effect
- Problem-Solution
- Narrative: Beginning, Middle, End
- Pro-Con
- Before-After
- Effect-Cause
- Long Shot-Medium Shot-Close-up
- Solution-Problem
- Past-Present-Future
- Least Important-Most Important
- Risks-Rewards
- Need-Solution-Action

Speech Outline Formats

The audience needs a logical sequence of events in order to follow and comprehend. No matter how you produce this, you as speaker must establish what it is we will tour; where specifically we are going, why it is important to know about it, how we can and what, if anything, we need to do about the information we gain.

There are two methods most speakers use to structure their presentations: The traditional outline and the use of more nontraditional methods involving figures of various kinds. It really does not matter what format you choose; what matters is what the audiences can see, hear, understand and feel as the result of the structure of your speech. The bottom line is this:

Are you clear?
Are you logical?
Can we follow you?
Do you make sense?
Do you provide structure?

Traditional Outline Format

There is no set way of making a speech outline. But we, as audience, need structure -- not randomness. So, no matter how we approach speech outlining we still are required to know our audience as best we can, know our topic and purpose, and provide structure. Many very successful speakers to achieve these ends use the following 7-step outline:

1. Analyze your audience
2. State a clear controlling idea (C.I.)
3. Choose 2 to 5 main points
4. Support and illustrate each main point
5. Write a conclusion
6. Plan and write the introduction
7. Plan and test transitions

Step 1: Audience Analysis. You must ask yourself these questions:

Who is my audience?
What do they expect from me?
What level of education is represented in my audience?
Why did they come to listen to me?
What will be their immediate environment?
What are their backgrounds, occupations, gender, ages?
What are their cultural issues?
What do they already know about my topic?

Until you complete an audience analysis as thoroughly as possible, you cannot expect to connect properly with that group. If you do not connect with your audience, you have probably wasted everyone's time and energy.

Remember: No connection = no communication.
We must connect with our audience on some level.
Do your homework.
Never underestimate the importance of audience analysis.

Step 2: State a clear controlling idea (C.I.). This is the core of your speech. Try to word your C.I. briefly. Focus on these questions:

What do I want to achieve with this topic?
If there is a single idea I want my audience
to remember, what is it?
What exactly do I want to accomplish with this speech?

The C.I. statement is the verbal map of the territory you will cover in the speech. You need to be clear about what you are discussing. If you are not clear on your C.I., how can you ever expect your audience to be clear on your C.I.? You cannot conduct a tour of a place you do not know and understand.

Step 3: Word your main points. The main points of your speech are the major concepts/ideas necessary for the audience's comprehension of the overall controlling idea. Depending on the time allotted for your speech and the complexity of your controlling idea, try and limit your main points to approximately three to five (At times, you may have to limit to just one!). Abraham Lincoln, in his "Gettysburg Address," used a 3-point outline that used the "past-present-future" logical pattern:

1. "Fourscore and seven years ago ..." (past)
2. "Now we are engaged in a ... " (present)
3. "... dedicated to the great task remaining before us ..." (future)

The triad (e.g., past-present-future, first-second-third, etc.) is an extremely useful tool for building main points. In fact, audiences tend to listen to and remember triads easily. Here is a list of sample triads incorporating the following visual model:

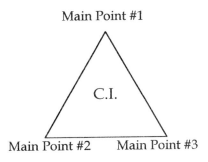

This visual triad has proven to be useful to those less successful with the linear approach (more on this later).

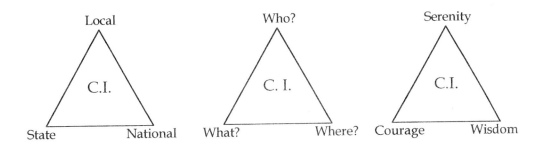

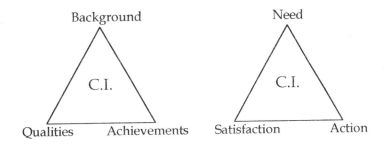

Step 4: Support for main points. A main point will usually require at least two forms of support in order to develop it. Actually, three points are better since one point could be chance. Our ideas stand on

more solid ground with a second and third form of support. Here is an example (see visual reference on page 75):

First, the controlling idea: Speech fright can be overcome by making three major changes.

Second, develop three main points.

Third, find at least two types of support for each main point. Here it is in traditional outline form:

I.   *Main Point 1: Thinking must change*
      A.   *Personal Experience*
                Research findings
      B.   *Descriptions*
      C.   *Quotations*
           1.   *experts*
           2.   *speech fright victims*

II.   *Main Point 2: Physical reaction must change*
      A.   *Explanation of stress reaction*
      B.   *Description of desensitization process*
      C.   *Demonstration of desensitization process*

III.   *Main Point 3: Habits must change*
      A.   *Examples of avoidance*
      B.   *New behavior during speech*
      C.   *Quotations*
           1.   *those who have changed habits*
           2.   *experts*

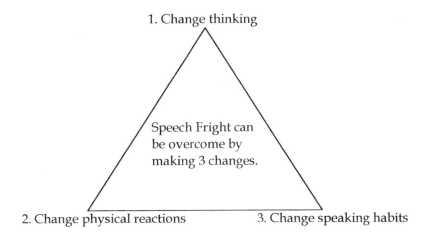

1. Change thinking

Speech Fright can
be overcome by
making 3 changes.

2. Change physical reactions   3. Change speaking habits

Step 5: Write a conclusion (see Chapter 8). This is where we concentrate all of our ideas together for one final impact. We formulate the conclusion at this time based on the controlling idea, main points, and the discussion/supports in the body of the speech. Here is a triad as a model for a conclusion:

1. Summary/Recap

2. Emotional appeal   3. Call for action

Step 6: Write an introduction (see Chapter 7). We usually wait until this point to design the introduction because, after the main ideas are developed, now we know what to introduce. The purpose of the introduction is to gain the attention of the audience, establish a relationship with the audience and lead into the topic.

The introduction can be successful in achieving its purpose by using one or more of the following devices (list not complete):

- Development of common ground
- Definition of terms
- Narrative (story)
- Rhetorical question(s)
- Quotation
- Use of humor
- Startling statement
- Statement of the topic or controlling idea
- Use of visual aids

Step 7: Plan transitions. The transition is a verbal bridge that takes the listener's attention from point to point. Be sure you know how you will move from:

- Introduction to body of speech
- Main point to main point
- Main point to supporting material
- Body of speech to conclusion

Transitions are often formed by using questions, repetitions, step-by-step progressions (e.g., one-two-three, A-B-C, etc.) and restatements. You might try one of these examples of transitional phrases:

"For instance ..."
"Let me explain ..."
"What does all of this mean?"
"This is shown by ..."
"As I said earlier ..."
"According to ..."
"What more can we do?"
"What can we conclude from these examples?"
"Last of all ..."

Transitions help keep the audience on the idea tour you are leading. They are the signals you give that you are finishing a point, starting a new point, thinking over what has been said or ending the idea tour.

Nontraditional Outline Formats

Here are some ideas for nontraditional speech development and organizational patterns. Not everyone is the same when it comes to being creative. Some of us learn best by visual means, some through hearing, some by doing or by touching.

For those people who are most comfortable with pictures, maps, schematics and the like, it may be useful to develop speech ideas graphically. Not all of us think first in strictly logical, linear, linguistic formats. The outline or paragraph forms may cause some of us trouble in the development of our messages for the enlarged conversation called public speaking.

Some
        of
            us prefer
                    different
                            patterns.

Some people

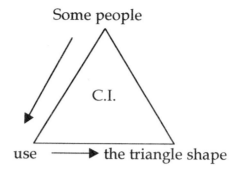

use → the triangle shape

Some people use

A star to guide them.

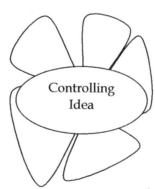

Some students have used this "free form" flower to guide them.

Left Brain/Right Brain

Humans have two brains (hemispheres) connected by a bundle of nerve passages (corpus callosum) which permit us to think in different ways. The **left brain** (hemisphere) is responsible for logical, linear and linguistic thinking. The **right brain** (hemisphere) is responsible for motor skills, emotion, music and spatial relationships. Those speakers who naturally choose the use of shapes, colors, diagrams, etc. to organize their ideas prefer their right brain.

The nerve connector (corpus callosum) allows us to switch back and forth between the two sides of the brain. Whichever our natural preference, we use both sides of the brain, shifting back and forth, depending on the skills needed.

Ways of thinking in our two "brains" might look like this:

Left Side: verbal (linguistic)
rational
goal-oriented
sequential
concrete
analytical

Right Side: nonverbal **symbolic**
EMOTIONAL physical
Holistic

Playful

Artistic

You might want to consider using the following steps which attempt to **combine both left and right brain** approaches for speech composition:

- ❑ Define your purpose. Ask, "Am I to inform, persuade, or both?" "Am I expected to entertain, challenge, inspire?" (left brain)
- ❑ Make a list of everything you think the speech will need; descriptions, personal experiences, statistics, quotes, humor, etc. (left brain)
- ❑ "Triad" your topic. Select 3 basic ideas you wish to present and put them in this form (both left and right brain):

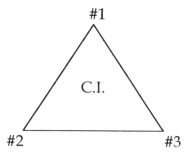

- ❑ Visualize your audience. Mentally ask your audience questions. Record the answers that come to mind. For example: "What do you know about my topic?" "How can I get your attention?" "May I use humor with you?" (right brain)
- ❑ Write out ideas about your speech that come to you automatically. Do not analyze any thought, just write it down. Allow time for this -- thoughts come at unexpected moments. (right brain)
- ❑ Rearrange your ideas. Develop a controlling idea and three to five main points taken from the previous steps. (left brain)

- Speak your material aloud to a listener you can visualize. Listen for logical progressions. (both right and left brain)
- Produce a finished copy of what you want to communicate in the form you find most usable. You may choose to write the speech out as a manuscript, you may outline, you may choose a figure upon which to "hang your ideas." (both left and right brain)
- Speak the speech to a friend. (both left and right brain)

Ideas to Aid Memory

Try these ideas to aid your memory when preparing for a speech:

- Associate new ideas or words with material you already know. Use analogies, comparisons, contrasts, paraphrases and metaphors to help you focus your memory on the speech ideas. (left brain)
- Visualize objects -- such as a book, a mirror, and a light bulb -- which represent main points to be covered. "Place" the objects in different locations in your home and "visualize" yourself moving from room to room to retrieve the objects. Tell the story/point about each object as you mentally pick up each object. (right brain)
- Use acronyms. Use each letter of a word to represent a major point in your speech (left brain):
  - Speech = How to prepare for a party
    - **P** - plan
    - **A** - artwork and decorations
    - **R** - reservations
    - **T** - table partners
    - **Y** - y'all come! (invitations)
  - Speech = Steps in cardiopulmonary resuscitation
    - **A** - airway (clear)
    - **B** - breathing (restore)
    - **C** - CPR (start)

This chapter is about organization of ideas. As tourguide, you must "plan the route" of the "idea tour" on which you take us, the audience. We stay on the trip longer and get more out of the trip if you take us in a logical, organized manner. Do not be afraid to try the different approaches to speech preparation, organization and memory techniques presented in this chapter. Find the method that works best for you and practice, practice, practice -- make the approaches your own! **No one sees your outlines, lists or pictures, but the audience *will hear* your organization and *will be better able* to listen and comprehend. When you are well prepared and organized you will do your most spontaneous, believable and fear-free speaking.**

Diversity Issues Regarding Planning the Route

1. Some cultures, like the greater Western culture, are linear in their thinking and logical development (clearly moving from one point to the next in a forward motion) while other cultures are more collective and circular in their logical development (bringing in the whole picture as much as possible which may involve what Westerners consider "back tracking"). How do these differences affect not only how we speak and listen across culture but also how we evaluate these messages?

2. Gender differences include logical ordering of ideas. Research this issue. How do these differences affect how males and females speak and listen in the public speaking setting?

Critical Thinking Issues Regarding Planning the Route

1. As public speakers, we have to speak to the audience as a whole -- which means we often have to speak to the majority without ever expecting to reach everyone. How do we manage this when the majority is clearly from a culture different from our own? What demands does this put on the speaker? What ethical considerations might come into play for us as speaker and as audience?

2. What are the ethical and moral considerations regarding the appropriate logical development used in the evaluating of culturally diverse public speaking classes?

Exercises: Applying the Chapter to Your Life

1. Rent and view films from cultures different from your own. As you watch the stories developing, note if you feel frustrated -- as if the story does not make sense. As best you can, note what is missing or added that is distracting you from understanding. Share your results with others in class. How does this transfer to listening and/or speaking in the public speaking context?

2. When preparing your next speech, force yourself to use a method of outlining that you have never before tried. Did you find this new method more or less productive? Why?

Selecting a Topic

Outside the classroom, the situation, the particular audience and their needs and the qualifications of the speaker will determine the speech topic.

In the classroom, you will probably have much freedom in choosing your topic. It is not unusual for students to develop a mental block when attempting to decide what to say in a speech class. The following guidelines will help you make a decision on a topic:

❑ What interests you?
❑ What experience have you had that is unusual?
❑ What special hobby or knowledge do you have?
❑ What subject do you wish to know more about?
❑ What is your work experience?
❑ How about your family?
❑ Do you or did you have a special animal friend?
❑ Have a favorite story?

If you are still having trouble, try the technique of brainstorming:

❑ Set a time limit (approximately 15 minutes)
❑ Record all thoughts (potential speech topics) without censoring yourself in any way – anything goes! Write your ideas quickly.
❑ Lay the writing aside for an hour or more -- let the **MESS-AGE**

❑ Read your topics. Select one and begin to work on it.

Whichever method you choose in deciding your topic – **START EARLY!**

If you are still having a great deal of trouble selecting your topic, I believe you are experiencing a form of speech anxiety. It is time to make an appointment with your instructor. Share your frustrations and ask for help. Together you will succeed in finding that special topic.

Chapter 7: How Do I Start My Speech? - Introductions

Paraphrasing an ancient Chinese proverb, a long journey begins with the first step. While this may seem trite, the first step is crucial: What if you trip? What if you start too fast or too slow? What if you step in the wrong direction? Well, the journey may not be as exciting, profitable or enjoyable as you had hoped. Your audience may agree.

As the "tourguide" speaker your initial contact with your audience gets them into the frame of mind of where you are going, the route you are going to take and why the tour is important to them (hopefully for reasons other than they have paid money for it). If you seem uncertain, bored or unwilling to "conduct the tour," then most likely your audience will be bored, uncertain, unwilling and unsatisfied with the time they have spent with you.

Introductions must:
- ❑ **Get the audience's attention**
- ❑ **Create a bond of good will**
- ❑ **Set the emotional and psychological tone**
- ❑ **Lead the audience into the content**

There is no particular order for these four elements -- that is the art of public speaking -- but experience shows us that these four elements are essential. The audience cannot follow your ideas if they are not paying attention. The audience must trust you in order to believe you. By setting the emotional and psychological tone, you prepare the audience for the appropriate mood. As tourguide, you then must lead the audience effortlessly into the main ideas of your speech.

How long should the introduction be? Long enough to put the audience in the frame of mind that will encourage them to listen -- and, of course, the shorter the speech the shorter the introduction. It is a common problem for beginning speakers and speakers who have high levels of speech fright to become over-involved with an introduction. It is as if too much attention is put on getting the audience to "like" the speaker. What often happens is that too much time is spent on establishing the mood and good will and time is then cut short for the body and conclusion. So, make certain that your introduction is long enough to fulfill its purpose while still allowing time to develop your central message. Typically, the introduction accounts for approximately 10-15% of the total speech.

When does the introduction begin? The moment your name is announced or the moment your audience lays eyes on you. Specifically, your introduction begins long before you utter your first words.

Remember:
Your introduction begins the moment
the audience is aware of you!

The moment the audience is aware of you, you are setting the tone of the event and building the bond between you and your audience. How do you look? How do you sound? How do you walk to the front of the room or get up from your chair? Are you excited? Happy to be here? Are you sure of yourself and your information? The first seconds of your presence can be as powerful as your first words. You may have the most influential or entertaining information possible, but if you present yourself as insecure, uninvolved, or not prepared, your information may be lost. At the same time, if you appear confident, interested and interesting, your information can actually become more powerful.

You can "make or break" your entire public speaking event in the first minutes of your speech. It is your responsibility to "set the stage" for your audience. Remember, in oral communication, especially public speaking, the listener has to be able to follow the speaker as he speaks. As listeners to oral communication, we do not have the luxury of rereading material. Make it easy for your audience to listen: Tell us where you are taking us on our tour, why it is important that we stay for the entire trip and connect with us as humans so that we believe that you are the most informed and trustworthy tourguide for us.

Preparing an Introduction

The following sections are designed to help you maximize your preparation of your introduction.

Audience Analysis

Before actually composing an introduction, it is wise to ask who your audience is and what they need to know about you and your topic:

- Do they know you?
- How much do you know about them?
- Are they familiar with your topic?
- How much background information will they need?
- Would humor or illustrations appeal to them?
- What cultural issues must you take into account?

Techniques for Building Introductions

The type of introduction technique used depends on your own personal style, the topic being introduced, the situation in which you are speaking and the personality of the audience. Here are some of the more effective ways of introducing your speech. Experiment with them until you find which is best suited for you and then adapt accordingly for each new audience, topic and situation:

- ❑ Use a startling statement: "Drugs are fun!" Then proceed to show how drugs kill and destroy people.

- ❑ Use a question or a series of questions: "Do you know the seven danger signals of cancer? You'd better -- not knowing the answer to this could kill you." Now you have the audience's attention! The next step is to inform them of the seven danger signals.

- ❑ Tell a story (narrative): "Not too long ago, a student, much like you and me, was involved in a horrible incident on campus ..." You have just piqued the audience's interest and connected us as a common group of people in a shared situation. If your story clearly illustrates your main idea and easily leads into your topic, you have an unbeatable introduction.

- ❑ Make a direct personal reference or statement to the audience: "Say, were you panting when you got to the top of the stairs this morning? I was. I'll bet there were a few of you who vowed you're never going to take a class on the top floor of this building again. But did you ever stop to think that maybe the problem isn't that this class is on the top floor of the building? You know it just might be that you and I are not getting enough exercise." This opening has an element of audience adaptation -- the personal reference is directed solely to that end -- it connects the audience with the speaker and the topic.

- Use a quotation: You might find a quotation that captures your controlling idea in a brief statement. **CAUTION:** Know this material well enough so you can quote it without losing eye contact with your group. This way you remain in direct contact and conversational with your audience. This enhances the power of the connection between you, the quote and the audience.

- Offer a preview of what you plan to cover: "During my time with you today I plan to show you the benefits of home exercise, the three most effective home exercises and how to plan a home exercise program." Just signpost the key ideas -- go into detail in the body of our speech. This technique is often referred to as the filmmaker's "long shot" (see Chapter 12). This approach establishes where you are going and what specifically will be discussed.

- Combine several of these elements: Nearly all introductions do. "Has anyone here ever experienced speech fright (questions)? When I gave my first speech in the sixth grade (personal reference), I entirely forgot my memorized manuscript and fumbled through with great embarrassment. Mark Twain once said ... (quote) ..." You will find that combining techniques can be especially powerful in:

  - Getting the audience's attention
  - Establishing a bond between speaker, audience and topic
  - Setting the emotional and psychological tone
  - Signposting the topic to be discussed

Further Tips for Introductions

When developing your introductions, keep the following ideas in mind:

- Remember to plan your introductory remarks as the **FINAL** step in preparing your speech. **AFTER** you know what you are covering in the main points of your talk, you can plan how to introduce yourself, your ideas and your information.
- Plan both your first words and your nonverbal behavior as you think through your introduction. **YOU ARE YOUR SPEECH.**
- What you **DO** speaks more loudly than what you say -- especially in the first moments of your presentation. Plan to walk with purpose, stand straight (not stiffly), smile (if appropriate to the tone of your talk), look at your audience and connect with them. Let your audience know that you are a human conversing with other humans. Let your audience know that you are sincere and there to share with them.
- It helps to remember you are the "tourguide" of your speech. You are responsible to build a bond of trust and credibility with the audience by showing them you are glad to be there, that you know what you are talking about, that you are interested in them and in what you are telling them. If you start in a faltering, fumbling, unclear way, the audience members begin to tune you out in the first few seconds. If we begin to think, "What's this about?," or ""This sounds boring!," or "Who cares?," then you may have lost us forever.
- What you say and do first is often most remembered. Look for material that will capture our attention. Help us relate to you and your topic and lead us easily into your "tour of ideas."

Chapter 8: How Do I End My Speech? - Conclusions

As the "tourguide" you have taken us on our "journey of ideas" and now it is time to bring our event to a meaningful end. Perhaps the *least effective* thing you can do at this point is to leave us wondering if there are any further ideas left to be uncovered or if, in fact, you have finished your communication with us.

You may have talked for five minutes or even an hour but when you come to the end of your ideas you have one last chance to put focus where you want it. The object of concluding remarks is to provide closure, a sense of completeness. What we hear last is often best remembered. Actually, there has been debate on what is remembered most -- that which is heard first or last -- but the fact remains that both first and last are crucial. That is why introductions and conclusions can strengthen or weaken your speech.

The conclusion, more than any other part of the speech, needs to be carefully planned because we get so little practice in concluding remarks in everyday speech. Most of the time we end conversations with statements like, "Got to go now," or "Good talking to you," or "This was fun, see you tomorrow!" In the enlarged conversation we call public speaking, however, we must do more than simply stop talking and move on. We have to provide true closure -- a sense of a completed package.

> **Conclusions tie together
> the key ideas and emotions
> presented in the
> body of the speech**

As audience, we yearn for both logical and psychological closure at the end of any presentation. We are rewarded when the speaker summarizes and helps us logically tie together the various main ideas of the speech. The speaker and the presentation also emotionally touch us when the conclusion helps us experience relief, anger, joy -- whatever is appropriate to the speech content. Martin Luther King, Jr. provided his "I Have a Dream" speech through the use of the words of an old spiritual, "Free at last, free at last. Thank God, Almighty, we are free at last." By quoting this, he tied to the universal of freedom while tapping into our immediate yearning for the same. I suggest you read his entire speech as an example of public speaking rising above the call of immediate communication and remaining a beautiful and powerful message for all time.

Preparing a Conclusion

As with introductions, the type of conclusion you prepare depends on your own personal style, the topic being discussed, the situation in which you are speaking, the personality of the audience and what points (logical and emotional) you want the audience to most remember. Experiment with the various techniques listed in this chapter until you find which is best suited for you and then adapt accordingly for each new audience, topic and speaking situation.

Techniques for Building Conclusions

The various methods for concluding a presentation can be summarized as follows:

- ❏ Summarize the main ideas. Recap the key ideas while tying back to the mood established in the introduction. For example, a speech on how to detect cancer would summarize the warning signals: "So remember, if you experience a sudden weight loss, lack of energy, blood in your urine or bowels, then you should see a doctor immediately. It is never too early to check out a potential killer -- so what if you were wrong? What if you were right?" The virtue of such an ending is that it restates the main points and puts those ideas into perspective for the audience.

- ❏ Connect your topic to larger issues. For example: "By developing a home exercise program you will enhance the quality of your life because you will stay healthy, be more mentally alert and will pay less for medical bills. And when you think about it, as the quality of your life increases, so does the quality of the lives of those who are closest to you because you can give more to and require less from them." This type of ending takes the single ideas of your speech and puts it into a larger whole, giving your topic a universal appeal.

- ❏ Show how the ideas you presented effect our life. For example: "By considering alternative automotive fuels we stand the chance of saving our air, creating more jobs, stabilizing the environment and becoming more economically independent. This means our economy will flourish and the overall health of our world will improve." This tells the audience just what effects your information or actions will directly have on them.

❑ Make a direct appeal. The appeal is a frequently used conclusion for a persuasive speech. It is as though you tell your listeners that now that they have heard all of the arguments, you will describe the behavior you would like them to follow. For example: "So, we've seen that Beulah Wordlow is dedicated, experienced and a creative problem solver -- that she would make a superior City Councilwoman. I hope that next Tuesday you will exercise your right to vote. But most important, I hope that you will vote for the best candidate -- Beulah Wordlow."

❑ Use emotional impact. This type of conclusion points out the most important idea(s) with emotional impact. Consider the powerful way General Douglas MacArthur finished his speech when he ended his military career: "But I still remember the refrain of one of the most popular barrack ballads of that day which proclaimed most proudly that 'Old soldiers never die; they just fade away.' And like the old soldier of that ballad, I now close my military career and just fade away -- an old soldier who tried to do his duty as God gave him the light to see that duty. Good-bye."

❑ Find a way to finish with a "zinger." A zinger, or clincher, is a final statement or exit line that leaves no doubt that you are finished yet continues to drive the key idea of the speech. Try these -- end with a:

> ❑ Question or series of questions: "Can we afford to do this? Can we afford not to? It's your decision -- isn't it?"
>
> ❑ Short narrative that restates your theme: "As Bill was driving home from school he was doing everything right as a driver. The drunk driver who ran the red light was making the mistakes. Nevertheless, Bill was hit broadside and nearly killed. He would have been killed had it not been for his seatbelt. You could be that careful driver, like Bill, who just happened to be

in the wrong place at the right time. Please, buckle up." This structured illustration is easy for the audience to follow.

❑ Statement of your own intent: "I plan to give blood tomorrow at the Red Cross. I look forward to seeing you there." This is very persuasive because you as the speaker identify not only with the audience but with the desired action as well.

❑ Bit of humor. Be careful with humor. Do not leave the audience feeling put down, let down or confused by your humor. Also, avoid changing the mood of your speech with humor, unless that is the effect you wish.

Further Tips for Conclusions

When developing your conclusions, keep the following points in mind:

❑ Avoid ending your presentation by falling into a weak statement of desperation: "I guess that is all -- uh, I've forgotten the last point," or "Thank you" as a substitute for an ending. This can confuse or frustrate the audience.

❑ Do not apologize as an ending by saying something like, "I guess I've gone on too long, so, well, uh, thanks." This type of ending weakens your total communication.

❑ Do not introduce a whole new idea in the conclusion. This can frustrate or confuse the audience.

❑ Keep the same style or mood that you established throughout the introduction and body of your speech.

❑ If you plan to use the phrase, "in conclusion" or "to summarize," use it only at the end of the final point. If you use such phrases in the body of the speech you create a false ending and may lose the audience's attention.

❑ The way we end our talk can be seen through the metaphor of "giving a gift." We wrap our ideas and provide direction for their use in our final words. We offer a personalized present for each listener to take home.

Chapter 9: Getting Conversational - The Oral Style

You have personal style. You and your style are unique -- because you are an **individual**. My objective is not to have all students of public speaking walking, talking and sounding alike. Not at all! I am hoping to heighten your awareness of your existing personal style while emphasizing what scholars know about communication style in order to present you with ways to improve and enhance your public speaking skills.

Your personal style is projected by the way you walk, talk, dress, move your hands, smile or laugh; by your attitudes toward your self and others. Your personal style includes the way you organize material; by the way you sound in conversation, reading aloud or speaking in public. Your style is your own style -- each of us has our own unique qualities. Yet as unique as we are, there are common qualities we must project to be successful in public speaking.

If I was able to ask you what made a successful public communication style, I believe you would come up with the following qualities:

- ❑ Naturalness
- ❑ Ability to dynamically show feelings
- ❑ Fluent (free from distracting vocal or physical habits)
- ❑ Trustworthy (credible)
- ❑ Spontaneous

Scholars in the field of public speaking generally agree upon these qualities describing a successful public speaker (Curtis, et. al, 1997, page 388). So, if you thought of any or all of them -- congratulations!

Where and when are we most spontaneous, natural, expressive of our feelings a well as fluent and credible? In our conversations! Yes, everyday conversation is the place to begin your study of public speaking. It is here in the familiar, spontaneous, one-to-one situation that we find most of the elements necessary for successful public speaking. We simply learn to enlarge them when we speak to a group of people.

Conversation is interaction. Conversation is at its best when it is idea-centered. Every conversational situation is different. In conversation, we usually do not know what our words will be; yet, we speak. We start sentences not knowing how or when we will end them. We reflect our feelings and our ideas yet we are not usually aware of individual words. Still, we voice our likes and dislikes, tell our story, and defend our positions. **WE INTERACT!** We speak, we listen, we adjust, and we communicate our ideas in a dynamic, alive manner.

Public speaking is enlarged conversation. When we speak in public we have more listeners, we speak longer without stopping for verbal exchange, sometimes we have to slowdown a bit and we must give more thought to overall organization of the message. It is still an idea-centered interaction we call, public speaking.

When you think it through, speaking is always public. The listener is there even if he or she is silent. Moreover, we have the same reasons or needs for speaking whether in conversation or in a more public, formal setting.

Conversation is something you do every day. This, then, is the place to begin to discover our personal public speaking style. You discover what works for you as a speaker within this arena. Conversation is the place to discover your habits of voice, speech, organization, body movement and facial expression that detract from your message. Conversation is the place to practice what works for us.

> **Conversation is the best and (often) only place to practice for the more challenging public speaking situation.**

It is in our daily conversations that we develop habits that go with us when we are called to speak in public. Whether or not we like it, our communication habits follow us wherever we speak. Our speech patterns can rarely be switched from ineffective to effective simply because we are called upon to speak in public. Yes, we can make minor adjustments (e.g., saying, "yes" instead of "yeah") but trying to adapt major vocal changes often creates self-consciousness and may create physical damage. Remember -- practice makes permanent, not perfect.

Conversational Speech Habits Inventory

Take a few moments to answer the following questions by circling either "Yes" or "No" after each question. The inventory is informative if you answer truthfully. All of these questions refer to your communication habits during conversation.

1. Do people often ask you to repeat? [Yes / No]
2. Do friends ask you to speak louder? [Yes / No]
3. Do friends ask you to speak softer? [Yes / No]
4. Do you clutter your speech with fillers ("right," "like," "an' stuff," "you know," "okay?") [Yes / No]
5. Do you fail to help your friends understand you by failing to use common experience or language? [Yes / No]
6. Do you use language that puts others down? [Yes / No]
7. Do you make general assertions but fail to support them with facts or examples? [Yes / No]
8. Do you fail to look at people when you talk? [Yes / No]
9. Do your listeners have trouble following you? [Yes / No]
10. Are you a gossip? [Yes / No]
11. Do you fail to summarize your ideas? [Yes / No]
12. Do you use a monotone voice? [Yes / No]
13. Are you too busy talking to listen? [Yes / No]
14. Do you fail to finish your thoughts -- jump from subject to subject? [Yes / No]
15. Do you fail to adjust to your listener's needs? [Yes / No]
16. Do people ever tell you that you sound phony? [Yes / No]

If you answered "Yes" to three or more of these questions, you need to analyze your habits and begin a program of improvement. Your instructor can refer you to someone trained in this area.

If your inventory indicates you need work on your everyday conversational habits, you can be certain that the enlarged conversation called public speaking will need improvement, too. Let us look more closely at what you can do to improve the elements of naturalness, fluid style and spontaneity in public speaking.

Causes of Unnatural Speech

The most common cause of failure to communicate naturalness in public speech is reading the entire speech. Most speakers are not nor will they become expert oral interpreters of the written word -- theirs or others. Furthermore, most of us actually resent being read to, especially if the reading is not on a par with the professional newsreaders we see and hear every day on television. Can you read like Dan Rather?

A second cause for sounding unnatural is the speaker who "puts on a show" by using dramatic gestures, exaggerated vocal variations and other obviously staged mannerisms. This kind of "performance" is a distraction to most audiences. While the broad "histrionic" style was popular in the early twentieth century, today's public speaking audiences expect a "slice of life" approach -- an enlarged naturalness -- not an artificial, exaggerated style.

The third reason for sounding unnatural is memorizing a speech, word for word. Many beginning speakers still believe they have to learn their speech like a singer learns a song. Wrong! All of us have listened to such a memorized performance and suffered along with the speaker who obviously does not understand that **public speaking is an interaction, a sharing, and a live relationship -- not a canned, one-way performance**. The memorized speech that just keeps going, no matter what, is an imitation of communication. Public speaking takes place in a REAL situation with LIVE people listening, interacting and adjusting.

The speaker and audience are joined in a verbal and nonverbal reality. The effective speaker is aware that his or her communication is happening NOW with THIS audience in THIS place -- never to be exactly reproduced. The memorized public speaker is isolated from the live interactive speech situation. The memorized speaker is really talking to an unseen audience in some unknowable time and place. This is not natural. When we are in an audience confronted by such a speaker, we know it, we hear it and respond by tuning out or by becoming fascinated by the "show" rather than hearing and thinking about ideas, issues or proposals presented. The reason for public communication is to "share ideas" not to "put on a show."

What You Can Do
to Develop Your Best Oral Style

What can you do to develop your best oral style? First, we need to understand that speech with another (or others) is always public -- in the sense that we are speaking with another human -- but not in content. That the best public speaking is an **enlarged conversation**: We speak, we listen, and we adjust. In public speech, we adjust by moving away from our prepared outline, talk with, and relate to the audience -- in the immediate -- **now**. We are not afraid to respond to the audience and the occasion. We know this is a live event and we adjust to it. We share, react and adjust in order to best communicate our ideas and fulfill our reason for being there. We project the naturalness of an enlarged conversation when we are at our best.

Another helpful way to achieve our own natural style is to include personal experiences and short narratives we can talk through without using notes or relying on a memorized "pitch." Even the most formal occasion benefits from the speaker's ability to relate personal life experiences, to elaborate an idea by personalizing it with humanistic examples.

Finally, and perhaps most important, we need to practice effective oral communication principles and techniques in our everyday conversation. Our conversations are our laboratories for experimenting, adjusting, clarifying and developing our own unique public speaking style.

Daily Checklist of Behaviors to Practice

- ☐ Stay idea-centered.
- ☐ Use simple language.
- ☐ Give clear references (let your listeners know who and what you are talking about by name, date, place, etc.).
- ☐ Do not be afraid to repeat important information.
- ☐ Ask questions of your audience -- frequently.
- ☐ Do not be afraid to express your feelings.
- ☐ Read and remember to use quotations from people who know their material.
- ☐ Listen to your audience.
- ☐ Look for common ground. Unless you share similar meanings for words you cannot communicate clearly.
- ☐ Check to see if you are understood (ask questions, look at the expressions on faces).
- ☐ Remember to "speak all over." Let what you are thinking and feeling be reflected in your face, body and hands.
- ☐ When you change topics use some transitional remark to alert your listener where you are going.
- ☐ Work to avoid fillers such as; "um," "ah," "and uh," "you know," "like," "and all that stuff," and "everything."
- ☐ Speak up -- do not drift into a monotone or drop off in volume so that the audience tunes out because they simply cannot hear you.
- ☐ Stay current with world and local news and share and discuss what is happening.
- ☐ Develop an area in which you can be an expert (music, sports, law, entertainment, politics, history, science, human behavior, etc.).
- ☐ Use proper grammar. The purpose here is not to be "stuffy" but to avoid habits that brand you are rude, careless or uneducated.
- ☐ Work on relating your experience in a clear narrative form (see Chapter 10). Storytellers are in demand as public speakers.

- Be assertive. You have a right to voice your opinions, ideas and feelings.
- Trust your unique ability to communicate your ideas clearly.
- Practice, practice, and practice -- daily; in every conversation, every meeting, every bull session, and every chance you get to converse with people.

Manuscript Speech Writing: Writing in the Oral Style

Speaking is not writing! Writing for the ear is not the same as composing for the eye. James Winans (1922) said, "A speech is not an essay on its hind legs." I believe he meant that an essay, no matter how excellent, will not necessarily be effective when read aloud to an audience. For one thing, we must grasp instantly what the speaker is saying -- we cannot re-read a speech! Most essays, on the other hand, must be studied to be comprehended.

Composition for speech also differs from the typical written composition because the speech takes place in a real situation. The occasion, audience and speaker all provide clues as to the speaker's meaning. The speech and the speaker form a nonverbal and verbal reality. Silences, pitch change, speed of speech as well as hundreds of other verbal and nonverbal clues all shape the communication which is heard, seen and felt by each person in an audience. Therefore, the words on the page are not the speech.

At best, the manuscript is a visual guide to help the speaker to be precise, colorful, or even poetic, if the occasion calls for it. Meaning is not in words. Meanings emerge from an interaction between speaker and audience. Meanings are in people. Yes, written language communicates but has different demands because it is assumed the reader has no live presence with whom to interact. The public speaker knows that her presence will be immediate.

Practical speech writing is a bit peculiar when we think about what we were taught in our literature classes and English composition courses. The following list contrasts what is effective for speech writing but might seem clumsy or substandard in an essay written for the eye. Effective composition for speech has more:

- Personal pronouns.
- Variety of sentences.
- Variety of sentence length. In spoken language, sentences are often one or two words or even sentence fragments used for emphasis or surprise.
- Questions.
- Repetition of phrases (creative redundancy such as "I Have a Dream" by Martin Luther King, Jr.)

- ❏ Monosyllabic (simple) words.
- ❏ Contractions.
- ❏ Slang or idiomatic expressions (as fits the occasion or audience to whom you will speak).
- ❏ Feeling language (connotation)
- ❏ Figurative language
- ❏ Direct quotes
- ❏ Familiar words
- ❏ Concrete use of references. "This" or "that," "him," or "her," -- any indefinite pronoun is dropped to avoid miscommunication.

The words and phrases must sound natural. A good speech can be said to sound like part of a good (enlarged) conversation. An excellent way to begin to achieve this kind of composition style is to practice writing then speaking your phrases aloud. If the tone is stiff, try substituting more everyday phrases and expressions. Shorten the sentences, use more questions -- get personal! Use "I," "you," and "we" freely. Use words that are more emotional and do not be afraid to repeat major information. Ask your audience to share your point of view. Be bold! As a public speaker you are, after all, a person and should come across as one.

We can build our speech writing style by refining both our vocabulary and our nonverbal habits of expression. We have to listen to ourselves, listen to others and listen for the "music" not just the "words" in oral communication. Style is the natural result of the way we think, feel and express our ideas orally on a daily basis. Work on your everyday speech. Take an upgraded conversational style into your writing and you will write well for public speech.

Chapter 10: Tell Me a Story - The Narrative Speech

"Tell me a story." Do you recall saying that when you were little? In addition, do you remember how satisfying it was to hear the story being told -- no matter how many times it was repeated? What was it you most liked about the story? Was it identifying with the characters? Being caught up with the action, adventure or mystery? Perhaps you learned a lesson or had a good laugh or cry over the events. Whatever it was, I hunch it was the drama of being taken on a journey which had a beginning, middle and an end -- a drama about life.

Sometimes the narrative, or story, is told in the form of a parable (such as "The Good Samaritan") or as a fairy tale (like "Snow White") or it can be a "fish story" (an exaggerated "real life" adventure). Walter Fisher writes, "Thinking in terms of stories ... is an essential way to relate to others, and is one reason human beings have been referred to as 'the story-telling animal.' " (Fisher, 1984, page 8) We find meaning in our experiences through sharing what has happened to us -- telling our story.

When you think of it, the story (or narrative) reflects the essential pattern of a public speech. The narrative has a beginning, middle and end. The introduction sets the tone, establishes the characters and often suggests conflict. The introduction is followed by one event after another, usually chronologically. Finally, the narrative comes to a conclusion or surprise ending or moral. The speech, too, has its beginning, middle and end (refer to Chapters 6, 7, and 8).

The narrative form can become, indeed, the organizational pattern of an entire speech. Because there is a logical progression built into a story as well as the need to know what happens, we find a pattern for a speech. The story form helps us structure our ideas in a dramatic way when we need to share our experience yet still make a point in the form of a life lesson, a moral or a new understanding.

A short narrative can also be used by a speaker as supportive or illustrative material in a speech. Some speakers use stories as opening attention-getting devices. Incorporating a narrative later in the speech to illustrate a point can also be very effective. In addition, concluding with a short narrative to bring focus and psychological closure for the listeners can offer that needed "clincher" with which to end.

Narratives can be used to inform, inspire, and delight and often to persuade others. A narrative always is concerned with telling "what happened." The speechmaker needs only to think deeply about an experience of his or her own or of another person to begin to develop a narrative speech. The following topics are examples of some of my former students' choices for narrative speeches:

- Travel to Mexico with Habitat for Humanity
- Travelling with my family across the sea in an overcrowded boat
- Surviving my parents' divorce
- Recovery from a killer disease
- Trying to get help in a country where I did not speak the native language
- Discovery of the "meaning of life" through travel
- Falling in love
- A most embarrassing experience and what I learned from it
- Coming to grips with my sanity while lost in the desert

- What led me to become a history major in college
- The first time I slept outside by myself
- My first date

How to Compose Your Narrative

Following are what I believe to be practical and effective steps for developing your narrative as part of the preparation process for your speech:

1. Develop and understand your theme. The theme of your story concerns the "why" of the narrative. This is the reason you are telling the story -- the lesson you learned, the truth you found, the way you now feel about the situation, the belief you developed, the change in your life, etc. Before you go to the next step, it is critical that you can formulate in your own mind the theme of your story.

2. Develop the story line. Lay out the sequence of events. Tell what happened while leading to a conclusion that shares what you learned, what changed how you now feel or a new attitude you have developed, etc.

3. Throughout the story, describe the characters. Show the audience what your people look like, how they think, their dominant attitudes and their mannerisms. Let us know what your characters sound like, dress like and how they relate to others: Are they frightened, bossy, kind, or patient?

Guidelines for Effective Delivery
of the Narrative

Telling a story does take practice to do well. Here are a few guidelines for effective delivery of the narrative:

- ❑ The story is best delivered with few notes. This is because the more direct your audience contact, the more powerful your impact.
- ❑ Notes should take the form of a word outline for essential names, events and phrases. This allows the speaker to maintain that all-important, direct audience contact.
- ❑ Do include dialogue. Try to use the words each character spoke with his or her tone and individual personality.
- ❑ Focus on the audience, not on yourself, as you attempt to share the experience as you remember it happening.
- ❑ Use simple, specific language to develop your characters and dramatize the events.
- ❑ Enjoy the power of your story to entertain, inspire, inform or even persuade as you help us understand and appreciate a common life experience. Your story will work if you prepare, practice and share with enthusiasm reflected in vocal variety, use of dramatic pauses and facial expression. Enjoy your story as you share "out loud."

Sample Outline of a Narrative Speech

An outline of a narrative speech might look like this. This outline and subsequent transcription (see sample below) was graciously offered for inclusion in this text by a former public speaking student.

I. *Theme*

> *I want to share with my audience my experience of running away from home and school. The lesson learned was that hitchhiking can be dangerous to your health and school is really the best place for a 15-year old girl to be.*

II. *CHARACTERS*

    A. *Myself*
    B. *Friend*
    C. *3 "Business-type" Men*
    D. *2 "Hippie-type" Men*
    E. *Silent Man*
    F. *Strange and threatening Man*
    G. *Police*

III. *EVENTS*

    A. *I sit with my friend before school*
    B. *I decide not to go to school*
    C. *We decide to hitchhike to San Francisco*
    D. *First ride*
    E. *Watts*
    F. *Second ride*
    G. *Ventura*
    H. *Third ride*

IV.   **CONCLUSION**

What we learned.

A.   *Hitchhiking can be dangerous*

B.   *School is the best place to be*

Sample Narrative Speech

The following narrative speech is the narrative written and delivered from the outline above. The individual who delivered the speech was enrolled in a beginning oral communication class. As you read it, listen with your "inner ear" for the sound of the spoken words. Ask yourself: "Did the speaker capture and maintain my interest?" "Did the narrative make its point?" "Can I identify with the speaker?"

It was February 14, 1967. I was 15 years old. That day I sat with my friend in Curry's Coffee Shop, drinking coffee and eating donuts, when I hear the school bell ring in the distance. Now I had been told if I missed one more day of school, one more class period of school, that was it; I was going to get kicked out. But I just couldn't face one more day in that oversized baby-sitting establishment when there was so much more to be learned in life. So there I sat across from my friend, Irene, looking intensely at her. Ahh, Irene was one of those soul friends. (Have you ever had a friend whose eyes you could look into and carry on a conversation without speaking? Well she was one of those friends.) We were looking at each other silently deciding what to do. As we sat, I blew a smoke ring across the table. The smoke ring floated across the table and circled Irene's turned-up nose.

Then it broke along her face. We just dissolved in laughter. We just cracked up. As the laughter ended, we got up from the table and somehow knew what we had to do. With the clothes on our back and 50 cents in our pocket we walked out into the street and put out our thumbs. We had decided right then, in 30 seconds, to go to San Francisco to see what the flower children had to say, to see if they had any answers.

Within 5 minutes after we started to hitchhike we got our first ride. The car contained three men, probably in their forties; all clean-cut business-type men. As we rode along, we found that they had given up their jobs and they had given up families and everything to see the country. They had just taken off. Well, we thought that was wonderful! I remember thinking, "Gee, I hope when I get that old I will be able to just drop everything and take off and see the world like this." They took us into an unsafe area of Los Angeles -- dropped us off.

Now this is not a real good place to be dropped off. The recent racial riots had just ended but violence threatened at every corner. You might say we were obvious outsiders in that area. As far as we could see, we were the only white teenagers standing around. We were also the only hitchhikers. And I'll bet we were the only girls whose knees were knocking out tunes all by themselves.

We stuck out our thumbs. A car stopped. We jumped in only to confront two men I'll never forget. One must have weighed 250 pounds and the other one had a "wild" hairdo out to here. He was just as skinny as a rail. After we were squeezed into the car, the man with the "wild" hair turned to us and said, "Hi, girls. My name is Ningo and you probably read about me in the newspapers." We said, "No. No, we haven't seen your name in the newspapers." I remember thinking; "I wonder who he killed?" Then our driver said to us, "I sure would like to take you girls around the corner and get you loaded." Irene and I looked at each other and I said, "Well, you know, this is our corner right here. But thanks, anyway." We jumped out of the car and ran and ran and ran.

We stood, gasping for breath, when a van stopped for us. Well, we knew that vans weren't a real safe thing to ride in but we were desperate. We jumped into the van and were confronted by a man who had long hair down his back, a scowl for a face, and the smell of buffalo. He grunted, "Where are you going?" We said, "San Francisco." He nodded his head and took off. He drove hunched over his wheel, in silence, all the way to Ventura. He never said a word to us. We sat, waiting for trouble. We rode like this all the way to Ventura. Without warning he slowed and stopped by this little shack on the side of Coast Highway. We were out in the middle of nowhere! It was drizzling rain. He said, "This is where I get off." He jumped out of the van and just kind of left us standing out there in the middle of nowhere.

I remember thinking as we stood there in the drizzling rain; "This is not good!" We waited and waited for what seemed hours for another car to stop and pick us up. A 1956, green and white Chevy finally stopped. This time we looked in at the driver before we jumped in. He was a good looking man, very clean cut, and I thought, "Good, at least here is someone halfway normal." So we jumped in the car. He seemed nice enough. His voice was mellow and his grammar revealed some education. He stopped and bought us cheese and wine because he discovered we had no money. Later, as we traveled along, he stared to tell us his story. He was, he said, on his way to San Francisco to go to court because he had been arrested on drug charges. He showed us a picture of himself before he had to get cleaned up for his court date. Irene and I gasped. In the picture, he had hair way down his back, a long beard, and was really hippie

114

looking. He offered us marijuana. (We thought that was kind of neat because we had never tried that before.)

But as we drove along, we realized there was something not quite right about this man. His car had a broken windshield and every so often he stopped by the side of the road to repair it -- always in the middle of nowhere, of course. He had a small machete and electrical tape and he sliced the electrical tape with that knife in order to repair the windshield. As he sliced the tape, he'd look at us and leer at us with a sick smile. Irene and I looked at each other and we knew that our time was limited. We knew we would never make it to San Francisco with this man. We were going to die before we got there. There was just no question in our mind. There was no place to go, no place to run. We were out on Coast Highway, out in the middle of nowhere. But we continued on with him. We had no choice.

Then, all of a sudden, flashing lights appeared. It was the police. They were looking for two runaway girls, coming from San Francisco and going to Los Angeles. We weren't the girls they were looking for, but we happened to be runaways, so we were taken to jail. Safe at last!

The moral of this story is, as Jiminy Cricket so succinctly put it, in the story of Pinocchio, "Think it through before you run. Don't be a fool. Stay in school."

Chapter 11: Share with Me - The Speech to Inform

When you choose to give an informative speech, your main purpose is to gain audience understanding, to share information with your listeners. Your specific purpose is to teach, instruct, clarify and impart "new" information about something. The effective informative speech encourages the "I didn't know that!" response from listeners.

An informative speech is necessarily characterized by:

- Accuracy -- derived from careful reading, research and study
- Completeness -- sufficient information to allow understanding of the subject
- Intelligibility -- clarity and organization of ideas which leads to interest and understanding
- Usefulness -- related to the audience's needs

Types of Informative Speeches

Informative speaking takes many forms. Listeners can be exposed to informative presentations of processes, instructions and directions. Informative talks also involve demonstrations and descriptions of objects. Informative speeches can also define a term, concept or value and can offer objective explanations of an idea, a theory, an issue, research or an event.

The diverse types of informative speeches fall into two practical categories: (1) those where the speaker is personally familiar with the process, procedure, and (2) those where the speaker must use outside source material to give depth to the speech.

The following paragraphs will discuss and provide guidelines for two major types of informative speeches, namely, demonstrations and descriptions. No matter which type of informative speech, remember:

Get the Listener's Attention!
Tell:
WHAT
HOW
WHERE
WHEN
WHY

Giving Demonstrations

Demonstration speeches are for showing how something works or how to do something. Specifically, the demonstration speech illustrates a process.

Sample topics for a demonstration speech include:

- ❏ How to load film into a camera
- ❏ How to shop for used cars
- ❏ Ways to plan a family budget

A particularly effective format for a demonstration speech is to:

1. Overview the process
2. Detail the process
3. Then, review the entire process for clarity

Consider the following guidelines when developing and presenting a demonstration:

- Everything hinges on the demonstration. If it does not work, neither will the rest of the speech. Make certain that you plan, practice, practice and further practice your demonstration.
- Backup equipment is necessary. Expect the worst to happen. Bring in an extra set of anything that is central to your demonstration (materials, bulbs for projectors, etc.).
- The "skip ahead" technique can be used. If the demonstration is a lengthy or complex process, you may want to have parts completed ahead of time so that you can skip the waiting period or lengthy (uninformative) process.
- Remind the listener of the purpose of the demonstration. In a demonstration dealing with the conditioning of mice in an experimental device (for example), the listeners can get so engrossed in the behavior of the mice that they forget what the demonstration is proving or showing. You will want to take a minute at the end of the demonstration to review the demonstration and relate it to the initial objective of the presentation.

Descriptive Speeches

The purpose of a descriptive speech is to describe an object or place, define a term or concept, or explain an idea.

Sample topics for a descriptive speech include:

- What is freedom of speech?
- What happened at the Battle of Little Bighorn?
- The effects of gillnets on the dolphin population.

A particularly effective format for a descriptive speech is to:

1. Overview the object, place or idea
2. Give specific information regarding the object, place or idea
3. Then, review the entire process for clarity

Consider the following guidelines when preparing for and presenting a descriptive speech:

- Choose an appropriate logical sequence:

  - Spatial -- begins at one location and ends at another
  - Chronological -- in order of time
  - Examples -- support your key ideas with examples, usually in order of importance
  - Compare/contrast -- focus on differences and similarities
  - Reasons -- explain by giving reasons for or against a particular viewpoint
  - Definitions -- describe by defining key terms
  - Effect to cause -- describe the effects that are the result of a problem
  - Cause to effect -- describe the problem that creates particular effects

- Visual aids will be very important in allowing your listeners to "see" what you are speaking.

❑ In an informative speech on definition, there are some methods for defining words (terms, concepts) that will improve the speaker's effectiveness:

    ❑ Give the historical derivation or development of the word

    ❑ Classify or categorize a word in order to define it. For example: Over the past several years there has been a considerable attempt to classify alcoholism as a "disease" both within and without of the medical profession.

    ❑ Use synonyms (words that have the same meaning) and antonyms (words that have the opposite meaning) as another way to define.

    ❑ Break a term into its various parts as a way of defining.

Preparing an Informative Speech

The planning and preparing of an informative speech falls into two categories: (1) gathering essential information, and (2) organizing the information.

Gathering Essential Information

When gathering information for your speech to inform, consider these guidelines:

    ❑ Analyze your audience. What do they already know about the topic? How often are they exposed to information on the topic? Consider:

        ❑ What new material do you bring to them via your speech?

- How much effort will have to be made to build your credibility during the presentation?

- Consider the situation:

  - How large is the room?
  - How many people will attend?
  - How many speakers will speak in addition to you?

- Research the topic.

  - Examine your own knowledge and experience
  - Ask friends and experts
  - Use direct observation, if possible
  - Read printed materials
  - Check the library
  - Always quote your sources
  - Allow time to think, incubate and create

- Establish your controlling idea. Decide on the controlling idea and express it in one sentence. If you do not know your goal, the controlling idea, you will not be able to logically and concisely build your message.

Organizing the Information

When the purpose of your public communication is to inform, let us, the audience, know where you are going -- follow a logical plan -- give us order. We need to have some sense of the whole picture before we can digest details.

The filmmaker (director) provides such a model for the speaker who wishes to inform. The filmmaker provides information in three parts: a long shot, a medium shot and the close-up. The long shot orients us to the big picture. What are the characters doing? Where are they?

Who is involved? The long shot gives us a general structure -- size, shape, color and what we are about to learn.

The medium shot fills in some detail. The speaker learns from the filmmaker that in this part the audience can be introduced to more information, can help us understand what is essential to learn and can intrigue us and move us to want to know more.

The next step is the close-up. Here the communicator gives us detail now understood from the previous background steps in the medium and long shots.

To provide conceptual understanding, the filmmaker then relates these medium and close-up shots to the entire story by returning to the long shot.

The idea of moving from general to specific and back to general is not limited to the filmmaker, but I use this illustration because we believe you can grasp the process by watching a movie or television show or newscast. You will observe the three steps clearly if you take time to analyze what the director is doing.

The reason I believe this process of movement from whole-part-whole works is that it makes sense to the receiver. We attend to a speaker when we can follow her logic. We can "stay with" the speaker who, first, provides us an overview of the material to be covered, then moves into some necessary detail for clarification, and then, moves to critical detail to provide learning and insight, and finally, puts all the detail back into perspective by relating it back to the whole.

If you view yourself as a tourguide of your special information, you will most naturally fall into the long shot, medium shot, close-up, and long shot organization. Show us the "city tour," the overview. Bring us along with the medium shot detail to the points of interest and then give us a close-up view of details as we peruse each stop along the way. When our tour is completed, remind us of what the "city" is all about in a new context.

If you speak to inform us, give us some organizational sequence or you risk losing us -- and we are all you have at this particular point in time. Even the newspaper gives us such a sequence by giving us a headline then developing the story and finally providing critical information needed to understand fully.

With this in mind, here is an informative speaking outline:

Controlling Idea: I want to inform my audience about ...

INTRODUCTON
(long shot)

I.	*Attention*	*(visual?)*
II.	*Purpose/ Importance*	*(visual?)*
III.	*Forecast of Main Points*	*(visual?)*

BODY

I.   *Main Idea*   *(visual?)*
(medium shot)

      A.   *Illustrative/Supportive Material*
               (close-up)

      B.   *Illustrative/Supportive Material*
               (close-up)

II.   *Main Idea*   *(visual?)*
(medium shot)

      A.   *Illustrative/Supportive Material*
               (close-up)

B.   *Illustrative/Supportive Material*
      (close-up)

      CONCLUSION
      (long shot)

I.   *Summarize highlights*
III.   *Draw conclusions/interpretations based on summary*
IV.   *Tie back to introduction*

Further Tips for Informing Others

- Supply new information. A speech to inform seeks to analyze, explain, report, describe or clarify some idea, issue, object, event or place.
- Establish the significance. Tell us why we need to know this information.
- Establish your authority. Speakers should suggest that they are well informed, using pertinent data or even rhetorical questions or other devices.
- Explain new ideas through reference to familiar ones.
- Avoid unnecessary details. The U.S. Air Force makes these suggestions to their personnel:

  - Underline the key sentences in your message and then condense these by eliminating "deadhead" words, by making one sentence do the work of two or three, by discarding unneeded illustrations and by making summaries of exact statistics.
  - Avoid hasty conclusions, wordiness and repetition.

- ❑ Direct yourself to the audience. You might try to find examples dealing with sports for one audience but your examples on another occasion might relate to music or family.
- ❑ Use special means to help the listeners remember. Use keywords, concrete examples, visual aids and other devices. If you, as a speaker, can move your listeners to see mental pictures of the ideas you are presenting just as you can move them to relate your ideas with certain ones they already have, they are most likely to remember.
- ❑ Avoid jargon. Use common terms.

Chapter 12: You Want Me to Speak Now? - The Impromptu Speech

We speak spontaneously to our friends every day. We are able to follow the topic, mood, or answer a question very naturally with little or no chance or need to preplan the conversation. Likewise, we respond spontaneously to questions in a job interview or when a teacher poses questions relating to the course we are studying. What is it we are doing in these situations? We are speaking impromptu.

The impromptu speech is that speech for which we have no time for formal presentation. It is the unplanned words and nonverbal communication we share in many situations:

- ❑ The classroom
- ❑ The job interview
- ❑ Reporting an experience to friends or family
- ❑ Describing an accident to a police officer
- ❑ Delivering a prayer at a church, synagogue, temple or shrine
- ❑ Clarifying points in a speech as a response to audience's questions
- ❑ Or, actually speaking impromptu in front of an audience

You are no stranger to the impromptu speech. Nevertheless, it still sounds scary, right? Perhaps it will help to remind you that you make impromptu speeches every day and that even the prepared speeches we have been discussing previously are compared to an enlarged conversation -- which is what most of the above-mentioned impromptu situations are. The prepared speech is in an oral style, is logical, is animated and spontaneous in delivery, and addresses issues and ideas of common concern between speaker and listener. So, too, are most conversations. So, too, are impromptu speeches. So, let us move on!

Impromptu speeches are like all other speeches in that they have:
- ❑ **A controlling/central idea**
- ❑ **Structure**
- ❑ **Logical and emotional elements.**
The only difference is that impromptu speakers have very little time for preplanning

---

Preparing the Impromptu Speech

Audience Analysis

As mentioned in previous chapters, before actually preparing any speech it is wise to ask whom your audience is and what they need to know about you and your topic. **Impromptu speeches are no exception!** Ask yourself:

- ❑ How much do I know about them?
- ❑ Do they know me?
- ❑ Are they familiar with my topic?
- ❑ How much background information do I already have?
- ❑ How much background information does my audience need?
- ❑ Would humor or illustrations appeal to them?

Organizing the Information

If impromptus are unplanned, how then do we prepare? First, we do not plan the words. Second, we do not plan delivery. Third, we do not try to plan specifics of what we will say.

What we can do is plan and begin to think habitually in terms of structure and personal experience. I will discuss the approaches I find successful for my students and myself. These include; the triad approach, the narrative approach, the flower approach, the filmmaker approach and the theme approach.

The Triad Approach

I find the triad structure to be most useful in impromptu speaking. The three-sided figure immediately suggests a way to break any topic, question or issue into three parts. I illustrate this point with a very common job interview question, "Tell me about yourself."

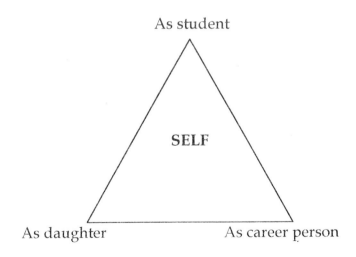

Most college students will find it logical and relatively easy to begin speaking about "self as student" because it is a familiar reference (e.g., with what you are now involved). Moving to the topic of "self as daughter" should be relatively easy by sharing some self-history. Finally, the student can then reflect on "self as a career person."

By breaking an unfocused, abstract request ("Tell me about yourself.") into three logical pieces, the speaker can rely on logic, her experiences and good conversational habits to see her through this impromptu request to communicate.

It is also relatively easy to add an introduction and conclusion to the triad above. For instance, the speaker may say, "That's a good question. Let me break it down into the following areas; myself as a student, myself as a daughter and my basic characteristics that will guide me as a career person." The conclusion could be a restatement of what was said or an attempt to highlight the strongest traits, work experience and academic achievements.

The triad approach can be used in many impromptu situations. First, ask yourself:

- What do I really know about this problem, situation, person, etc.?
- How can I break what I know into three logical points?

Once the subject is subdivided, you can speak about each of the three aspects of the issue as you would in a vital, animated conversation with a friend.

The Narrative Approach

Another useful way to approach organizing the impromptu speech is to use our old friend, the narrative. Often a request to speak will stimulate a memory of a personal experience, the experience of friends or family, or even something we have seen on television or read. Tell a story to illustrate your point, to answer a question, or to respond to a request, for example. A narrative can be a one-point speech that becomes a very effective response to the demands of a spontaneous communication situation.

The Flower Approach

If you have a few minutes to prepare your remarks, the following "free form" flower figure can also help to organize your thoughts. Use the "flower" to organize your thoughts in a logical progression (write notes in each of the petals). The flower also can provide a "visual anchor" to help you remember your logical progression as you speak. You can visualize the flower, thus keeping yourself on track. If the speaking situation deems it appropriate, for example, we can discuss: (1) *what* the topic is, means or implies, (2) *how* it will affect us, (3) use an example of *who* is for or against the topic, or who is involved or affected, (4) *when* the issue or its effects will be of most concern, and (5) *where* we might find more information concerning the topic.

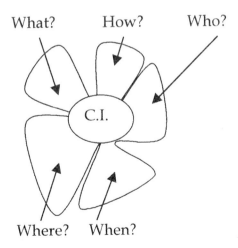

The Filmmaker Approach

You might use the filmmaker's approach to develop your thoughts on a given topic (discussed in detail in Chapter 11):

Long Shot (overview)
Medium Shot (introduction of specific ideas)
Close-up (details elaborating the ideas)
Long Shot (review)

I was asked to introduce a student I had met and interviewed earlier that day. I chose the filmmaker's organizational approach to meet this impromptu challenge. Here is an outline of what I said:

Long Shot: Statement of enjoyment in getting to know (name of student). A description followed of what I saw as a first response to this person.

Medium Shot: Three key characteristics were discovered; quiet, bright and sad.

Close-up: Elaboration of key characteristics:

QUIET -- She considers herself as shy. She comes from a small town in New Hampshire where talking is considered "showing off."

BRIGHT -- She is in college on a merit scholarship, majoring in Chemistry with a GPA of 3.8 (on a 4.0 scale).

SAD - She reveals her father died six months ago and she believes she is still working through her grief. We discussed the importance of sharing some of her feelings with others and she committed herself to developing a speech on the mourning process for her public speaking class.

Long Shot: The conclusion was a review of what I had learned and how this person had emotionally touched me.

By the way, I was given approximately three minutes to prepare -- a typical amount of time when dealing with impromptu speaking.

The Theme Approach

The theme approach has proven to be quite successful as a guideline in quick mental composition of the impromptu. Follow these steps:

1. Pick your theme (air pollution, gang warfare, love, marriage, family, politics, etc.).
2. Choose a way to organize the theme (for example):

   ❑ Pro-Con
   ❑ Problem-Solution
   ❑ Past-Present-Future
   ❑ Cause-Effect

3. Open the talk with an analysis, story or current experience relating to the theme.
4. Conclude with a restatement or summary of what you said.

Further Tips on Impromptu Speeches

I have previously compared public speaking to conversation by using the metaphor; public speaking is enlarged conversation. The impromptu speech may be the best example of an enlargement of speaking in the person-to-person setting and of carrying the best aspects of interpersonal communication into the public speaking setting.

When called upon to do an impromptu speech:

- **Do not panic!** When you are called upon to speak, remember you do this kind of speaking all the time. Take a deep breath, and
- Trust yourself to know how to organize, start and conclude a short discussion on any topic with which you are familiar.
- Ask for time. Especially in an interview setting, call for a rephrasing of the question or issue to gain time, if you need it, to think.
- Do not "wing" it as a substitute for preparation! Use the impromptu speech only when you do not have time to prepare more adequately -- when the situation is thrust upon you. Audience expectations in an impromptu setting are somewhat different from a formalized public speaking setting. To "wing" it, or speak unprepared in a formal setting can be devastating because the audience is assuming you have had time to prepare.
- Rely on your personal experience. Information from personal observation is better remembered and lends itself to an impromptu speech.
- Tell us a story. Whenever possible use a narrative, if it is clearly related to illustrate a point or to become the entire focus of your response. The narrative has the advantage of having a natural beginning-middle-end structure that helps

to keep us organized and to lead an audience through our thought process.

- ❏ Do not apologize. Your audience will know this is a surprise for you. They will have realistic expectations of you. Do the same for yourself.
- ❏ Use a quotation. A quotation can illustrate and organize your thoughts. An example might be to use the line from Dickens' (*Tale of Two Cities*), "It was the best of times, it was the worst of times. It was the summer of hope, it was the winter of our discontent" to describe the impromptu topic focusing on a major reorganization within your workplace.
- ❏ Keep it short. Try to speak as concisely as possible, avoiding generalities and repetition.
- ❏ Speak slowly and with purpose. Work toward a planned ending sentence or summary statement.

Chapter 13: Convince Me - The Speech to Persuade

Persuasion is not a mystical tool used by a select few . We **ALL** use it, **EVERY DAY**. Because of our prior experiences, persuasion may be a word that instills fear in us. We may have been led to believe that the persuasive process is complex and difficult for all except the most practiced writer or speaker. While the theory of persuasion is complex, I do not believe that successful persuasion is only limited to select individuals. Successful persuasion can be accomplished through a basic understanding of the process and practice in persuasive speaking skills.

A commonly held belief among many communication specialists is that every time we speak we attempt to change, stimulate or convince another person. I concur with this observation. Because of this belief, we can say that communication is a consistent attempt to persuade. We need to, therefore, study this way of speaking to objectify what we already do well as speakers and to discover better ways to influence other people, especially when we speak to an audience.

When we look at the field of persuasive speaking, we discover that it has been under study since 336 B.C. That is twenty-four centuries! Today, as in ancient times, the salesperson, teacher, politician, preacher, manager, media and medical professional use persuasive techniques in their careers. All of us need to become better consumers, or listeners (processors), of persuasive messages in order to make effective decisions in everyday life.

The Greek philosopher, Aristotle (336 B.C.), was the first to observe that persuasion was at once an art and a science. He wrote in his *Rhetoric* that persuasion was based on ethos, pathos and logos. In modern times, we still agree with this analysis but we use different language to describe the three parts; namely, credibility, emotion and reason. We see examples of these persuasive elements everyday in media advertisements and newscasts.

Ethos was the word Aristotle used to refer to the character, or credibility, of the speaker. We tend to believe the speaker we deem as worthy of our trust. For example, we believe a spokesperson for a product when we view that person's reputation or experience as trustworthy or appropriate.

Pathos was Aristotle's word for emotion. Emotional appeal is very much a part of the process of convincing another person to make a decision based on how the listener is influenced to feel. For example, many individuals have donated money to a particular cause because they felt compassion, fear, or perhaps guilt toward the cause or situation. The persuasive speaker appeals to our emotions.

By logos, Aristotle referred to the use of reason, evidence, or facts to convince a listener. We, as listeners, will often be convinced if enough evidence is given to support an action. For example, if compelling statistics are given to prove that more people who smoke die of lung cancer than those who do not smoke, then individuals may be convinced to try to stop smoking.

We observe that effective modern persuasive speaking does involve the conscious use of reason, emotional appeal and the credibility of the speaker to convince the listener to change a behavior, believe an argument, or maintain an existing attitude or behavior. The more a speaker can establish all three (reason, emotional appeal, and credibility) the more successful is the persuasion.

> ## In all persuasive speaking,
> ## we attempt to:
> ## change behavior,
> ## maintain behavior,
> ## or stop behavior.

The bottom line in persuasive speaking is to encourage action, to promote a specific type of behavior; be it observable, like voting for a specific candidate, or unobservable, like changing our belief about alternative automotive fuels. We are successful persuaders, convincers, when a belief is changed, when a desired action is actualized -- when the behavior is acted out.

The most effective way to move a listener to action is by tapping into the listener's needs. Abraham Maslow developed the following hierarchy of needs universal to humans: (1) **physical**, the most basic need; we need air, water, shelter, food and sleep in order to survive, (2) **safety**; we need to feel safe from war, nature, accidents and violence, (3) **social**; we all need to belong in relationships, to be able to influence and care for others, as well as be influenced and cared for by others, (4) **ego**; we have the need to believe we are worthwhile individuals, valued for who we are and what we do, and (5) **self-actualization**, the highest level need; the desire to develop our full potential as an individual. The effective persuader appeals to these needs (see *Audience Analysis*, which follows this section).

Here are some sample topics for a persuasive speech followed by the need being addressed:

- ❑ Wearing seatbelts in a car should be mandatory (safety need)
- ❑ Vote for the Clean Air Bill in order to keep our air safe (physical need)
- ❑ Continue your successful workplan in order to move ahead in the organization (ego need)

139

- Consider the effects of ultraviolet rays on your skin (safety need)
- You only life once! Live life to your fullest potential (self-actualizing)

While the bottom line to persuasion is action, the path toward achieving that action is through the audience's beliefs, values and attitudes. This is because these influence our behaviors. There is a connection between our beliefs, values and attitudes. Experts today dispute how direct these connections are but there is agreement that a connection does exist.

Simply, a belief is the acceptance that something exists, a value is the degree of importance that something holds for an individual, and, an attitude is the degree to which that something is liked or disliked. For example, an individual might believe in the concept of freedom of speech (belief) and hold that concept as so important in her life (value) that she strongly dislikes (attitude) anyone who keeps her from expressing herself, and therefore, is willing to enlist in the military (behavior) and risk her life to fight in a war (behavior) against a country attempting to squelch her freedom of speech. Another individual may share her belief in freedom of speech but may not value it as highly and, hence, may argue the validity of enlisting and risking his life for such a belief. These two individuals share an identical belief but their values, and hence, behaviors differ.

Our beliefs, values and attitudes are complex and are intertwined layer upon layer in our total belief system. It is imperative that we understand as best we can the belief system of our audience.

Preparing a Persuasive Speech

Audience Analysis

The very first step in preparing a persuasive speech is to analyze your audience. One way to understand your audience is to realize that we all have certain basic needs. The effective persuader develops a common ground with the audience by tapping into these universal needs. One technique for doing this is to list the experiences that the group you are to speak to is likely to have had. Find the key needs and experiences that relate to your topic. Use these shared experiences to help shape your persuasive message.

As a speaker, you also need to determine to what degree the audience is hostile, neutral or favorable toward your topic or issue. Ways to determine this may be through interviews, surveys, published reports, your past experience with the audience or information gained through networking. Be as thorough as possible in your audience analysis.

**Failure to understand your audience
may alienate you from your audience
and this will result in disaster.
Do not assume you know your audience.**

Sprague and Stuart (1998) give these guidelines when planning a persuasive speech:

- ❑ If your audience is **hostile** (strongly, moderately or slightly disagrees) toward your issue; stress common ground, base your speech on sound logic and extensive evidence. Pay particular attention to establishing a credible image.

- If your audience is **neutral** (neither agrees or disagrees) toward your issue; raise the audience's interest in your topic, emphasize material that clarifies and illuminates your position, and establish your credibility by presenting new arguments that blend logical and emotional appeals.
- If your audience is **favorable** (moderately, slightly, or strongly agrees) toward your issue; make use of emotional appeals to intensify your audience's support, get your listeners to make a public commitment, provide several alternatives of action, and prepare your audience to share your message with others.

Proofs

A proof is a tactic. Different tactics persuade people. What convinces one person may not impress others as effective proof. The wise speaker uses different kinds of proof to prompt the audience to change attitudes or act. I believe the most effective forms of proof are, but not limited to:

- Statistical evidence. Statistics are most effective when simple and easy to understand when spoken. Analogy often helps with large numbers. For example, if warning about the increasing national debt we can make the large number clear and real by showing that the interest alone each year costs each man, woman and child $1,800. Be careful with statistical evidence -- numbers may be out of date, taken from unrealistic surveys or discussed out of context.
- Narratives. Stories have power. The narrative makes examples come alive and easy to recall. Be careful with stories. They may or may not be grounded completely in truth.
- Testimony. Testimonies are opinions. Testimony adds to our credibility if we can cite a well-known expert to support our idea, candidate or product. Make certain that the

testimony comes from an individual who is an expert in the area being discussed. Do not assume titles indicate expertise. *Dr.* Smith may be, for example, a dentist, a professor, or a physician. In addition, she may be a heart specialist who is giving her opinion on liver cancer.

❑ Visual evidence. As we have heard many times, "a picture is worth a thousand words." For example, if you were attempting to convince an audience to consider plastic surgery, a video illustrating the "before" and "after" results (and, perhaps, the outpatient procedures) would provide vivid proof to make or reinforce the issue. Question, however, whether the video patient is representative of the majority of patients, and, whether or not the video illustrates the complete picture.

❑ Comparison and contrast. Comparisons and contrasts help us to see a problem from two perspectives rather than just one. Comparisons help to show relative similarities between things being compared, while contrasts point out differences. Be certain that what you compare and contrast really are probable candidates for these processes. Sometimes we attempt to compare items that are, by nature, incomparable.

❑ Analogy. An analogy is a form of proof that compares an unknown object with a known one. By comparing and contrasting key elements, the unknown object becomes familiar to us. For example, "The circulation of money is a important to the economy as the circulation of blood is to the body." The same cautions hold true here as in comparisons and contrast.

Organizing the Information -
The Motivated Sequence

One of the most useful ways to begin to develop effectiveness with persuasion is to learn to follow a pattern of organization first suggested by Monroe and Ehninger (1986) called the motivated sequence. This organizational pattern blends the logical approach with the psychological factors of attention, need satisfaction, visualization and action.

When we have to make a decision or solve a problem, we tend to go through a series of predictable steps:

1. We focus our attention on a single problem and reduce distractions.
2. We feel a need to change an undesirable situation, attitude or behavior.
3. We need to be convinced that a given change is correct -- that it will produce a better and workable solution.
4. We must be motivated to want to act on the proposed change. We must want to change a situation or attitude before moving to Step 5.
5. We actually make the change -- take the necessary action.

The persuasive speaker moves an audience through these steps by:

- ❑ focusing the audience's attention on a single issue, attitude, belief or problem,
- ❑ showing the need for change,
- ❑ giving sound evidence on why this change is logical and workable,
- ❑ stimulating us to want to do something about this issue, and, finally,
- ❑ Showing the audience what action will bring about this needed change.

A persuasive speech that uses the motivated sequence is organized in the following manner (Note: the subpoints are suggested choices, not all elements need be incorporated although you may choose to use several at any time):

I.   **Attention**

    A.   An example, illustration or story.
    B.   A humorous anecdote that makes a point.
    C.   A quotation that expresses a key point to be developed.

II.   **Need**

    A.   A direct statement that describes an undesirable situation that could be improved or strengthened.
    B.   An illustration that describes one or more detailed examples showing that the problem stated is actually a fact.
    C.   Further development that describes additional examples, instances, statistical data and testimonies that show how serious and widespread the problem is.
    D.   A relationship that explains how the problem affects the members of the immediate audience.

III.   **Satisfaction**

    A.   A direct statement of the action proposed to meet the need established earlier.
    B.   An explanation of the proposed action and what is involved in removing the problem by using the method suggested. The use of diagrams and other kinds of visuals should be considered.
    C.   A theoretical demonstration that explains how the proposed action would solve the problem.

D. A practical experience that provides support by giving real examples and instances in which such a proposal has solved the problem elsewhere.

IV. Visualization

People are more inclined to adopt a new course of action when they are imaginatively carried into the future to visualize conditions, as they would be when the action is carried out.

V. Action

The primary objective is to end the presentation with a sense of completeness that stirs the audience to action. Some of the most effective endings are these:

A. Summary, challenge, and a direct request to act.
B. A quotation that implies the action to be taken.
C. An example that suggests the action be taken.
D. An inducement. Salespeople use this approach when they give prizes or gifts for buying.
E. Testimony that indicates you are committed to the action and are accepting the proposal yourself.

Example Persuasive Speech Outline

Using the outline listed above; here is a persuasive speech outline for wearing seatbelts while riding in a car:

Purpose: *I want to change your attitude about wearing seatbelts in a car -- that you will wear them at all times, no matter how brief the trip.*

I. Attention

Focus attention on the issue by sharing a personal experience (narrative) of any injury accident in which the seatbelt saved my life.

II. Need

Establish the need to change by showing advantages (prevention of injury) and emphasize how easy it is to "buckle up." Show a very short film (video) illustrating the impact of accidents on passengers (adults and children) with and without seatbelts (available from police departments, trauma societies or college libraries).

III. Satisfaction

Emphasize the statistics on trauma and death due to unbelted accident victims. Emphasize the statistics on lack of trauma and death due to belted accident victims.

IV. Visualization

Appeal to the audience to save the lives of friends as well as their own by "buckling up" (motivate them to want to change). Again, share the story related in the introduction emphasizing that according to the police report, had I not been wearing my seatbelt, I would not be here to speak with the audience -- I would be dead.

V. **Action**

Ask the audience to a trial week of "buckling up" to change the habit of using seatbelts at all times in a car. Ask the audience to act as if the car will not start until the seatbelts are buckled.

Further Tips for Persuading Others

Remember that there is no guarantee that you will convince an audience to behave differently -- behavior is the result of a very complex system of beliefs, values and attitudes. Your success will be enhanced, however, if you remember these steps:

1. Know as thoroughly as possible your audience's stance on your topic of persuasion before planning your speech.
2. Incorporate reason, emotional appeal and your own credibility as sources to convince.
3. Provide your audience with a sequence of information that will motivate them to accept your suggestion:

   a. Get their attention,
   b. Establish that your topic is in need of consideration or change,
   c. Show how the problem or need can be satisfied, then
   d. Show how your proposed solution or action will actually look or work, and finally,

e. Provide a realistic course of action for your audience to take. Ask them for their commitment to follow through on your request.

4. Be prepared to spend a great deal of time preparing. To accomplish Steps 1, 2 and 3, you must give careful thought and planning time. If the topic of persuasion is of high value to you, and you believe that it should be of high value to your audience -- then the time is well spent.

Resources

_____. *The Rhetoric & The Poetics of Aristotle.* New York: The Modern Library, 1954.

_____. *Vital Speeches of the Day.* Mount Pleasant, South Carolina: City News Publishing Co.

Adler, R. B., Rosenfeld, L.B., & Towne, N. *Interplay: The Process of Interpersonal Communication, 4th edition.* New York: Holt, Rinehart and Winston, Inc., 1989.

Applebaum, R. L. & Anatol, K. W. E. *Strategies for Persuasive Communication.* Columbus, Ohio: Charles C. Merrill, 1974.

Beebe, S. A. *Public Speaking.* Boston, Massachusetts: Allyn and Bacon Publishing, 1996.

Birdwhistell, R. L. *Kinesics and Context.* Philadelphia, Pennsylvania: University of Pennsylvania Press, 1970.

Blakeslee, T. R. *The Right Brain.* Garden City, New York: Doubleday, 1980.

Buss, A. H. A conception of shyness. In J. A. Daly & J. C. McCroskey (Eds.), *Avoiding Communication.* Beverly Hills, California: Sage Publications, Inc., 1984.

Curtis, D. B., Floyd, J. J., & Winsor, J. L. *Business and Professional Communication. 2nd edition.* Dubuque, Iowa: Kendall-Hunt Publishing Co., 1997.

D'Angelo, F. A. *Conceptual Theory of Rhetoric.* Cambridge, Massachusetts: Winthrop Publishers, 1975.

Edwards, B. *Drawing on the Right Side of the Brain.* Los Angeles, California: J. P. Tarcher, 1979.

Ehninger, D., Gronbeck, B. E., McKerrow, R. E., & Monroe, A. H. *Principles and Types of Speech Communication. 10th edition.* Glenview, Illinois: Scott, Foresman, 1986.

Elbow, P. The shifting relationships between speech and writing. *College Composition and Communication*, 36, 1985.

Fisher, W. Narration as a human communication paradigm: The case of public moral argument. *Communication Monographs*, 1984, 51, 8.

Glaser, S. R. Oral communication apprehension and avoidance: The current status of treatment research. *Communication Education*, 30, 1981.

Goffman, E. *The Presentation of Self in Everyday Life*. New York: Doubleday, 1959.

Gundykunst, W. B. & Kim, Y. Y. *Communicating with Strangers: An Approach to Intercultural Communication. 2nd edition*. New York: McGraw-Hill, Inc., 1992.

Gundykunst, W. B., Ting-Toomey, S., & Nishida, T. (Eds.) *Communication in Personal Relationships Across Cultures*. Thousand Oaks, California: Sage Publications, 1996.

Guth, H. P. *New English Handbook, 2nd edition*. Belmont, California: Wadsworth Publishing Co., 1985.

Hart, R. P. et. al. *Public Communication*. University Press of America, 1987.

Jaffe, C. I. *Public Speaking: A Cultural Perspective*. Belmont, California: Wadsworth Publishing Co., 1995

Janis, J. H. *Writing and Communication in Business. 3rd edition*. New York: MacMillan, 1978.

Klopf, D. W. *Intercultural Encounters: The Fundamentals of Intercultural Communication. 4th edition*. Englewood, Colorado: Morton Publishing Company, 1998.

Knapp, M. L. *Nonverbal Communication and Human Interaction*. New York: Holt, Rinehart and Winston, 1978.

Larson, C. U. *Persuasion: Reception and Responsibility. 8th edition*. Belmont, California: Wadsworth Publishing Co., 1997.

Littlejohn, S. *Theories of Human Communication. 5th edition*. Belmont, California: Wadsworth Publishing Co., 1996.

Lucas, S. *The Art of Public Speaking. 6th edition*. New York: McGraw-Hill Publishing Co., 1997.

Lustig, M. W. & Koester, J. *Intercultural Competence: Interpersonal Communication Across Cultures. 2nd edition.* New York: HarperCollins College Publishers, 1996.

Maslow, A. H. *Motivation and Personality.* New York: Harper & Row, 1954.

McCroskey, J. C. & Richmond, V. *The Quiet Ones: Communication Apprehension and Shyness.* Dubuque, Iowa: Gorsuch Scarisbrick Publishers, 1980.

Mehrabian, A. *Silent Messages.* Belmont, California: Wadsworth Publishing Co., 1971.

Oliver, R .T. *History of Public Speaking in America.* Boston, Massachusetts: Allyn and Bacon, 1965.

Schutz, W. *The Interpersonal Underworld.* Palo Alto, California: Science & Behavior Books, 1966.

Scollon, R. & Scollon, S. W. *Intercultural Communication.* Oxford, UK: Blackwell Publishing, 1995.

Shimanoff, S. B. *Communication Rules: Theory and Research.* Beverly Hills, California: Sage Publications, 1980.

Spitzberg, B. *Handbook of Interpersonal Competence (Recent Research in Psychology Series).* Spr-Verlag Publishing, 1988.

Sprague, J. *The Speaker's Handbook. 5th edition.* San Diego, California: Harcourt Brace Jovanovich, Inc., 1998.

Stacks, D. W. & Stone, J. D. An examination of the effect of basic speech courses, self-concept and self-disclosure on communication apprehension. *Communication Education,* 33, 1984.

Teays, W. *Second Thoughts: Critical Thinking from a Multicultural Perspective.* Mountain View, California: Mayfield Publishing Co., 1996.

Welsh, J. J. *The Speech Writing Guide.* New York: Wiley, 1968.

Whiting, P. H. *How to Speak and Write with Humor.* New York: McGraw-Hill, 1959.

Wilmot, W. W. *Dyadic Communication. 3rd edition.* New York: Random House, 1987.

Wilmot, W. W. *Relational Communication.* *4th edition.* New York: McGraw-Hill, 1995.

Winans, J. A. *Speech Making.* New York: Appleton-Century-Crofts, 1922.

Wolvin, A. & Coakley, C. G. *Listening. 5th edition.* Dubuque, Iowa: Brown & Bushmark, 1995.

Wood, J. T. *Gendered Lives: Communication, Gender, and Culture. 3rd edition.* Belmont, California: Wadsworth Publishing Co., 1999.

Speech Anxiety
Follow-up Analysis

U se this form to track your speech anxiety symptoms. Complete the form as soon as possible following your public speaking experience. Share the information with your instructor or school counselor. Together you can work out a plan to minimize the symptoms.

Date of speaking event: _____ Time of speaking event: _____am/pm

Place: _____

Number of people in the audience: _____ Describe the audience: _____

_____

_____

What did you _most_ like about your speech? _____

_____

What did you _least_ like about your speech? _____

_____

Did you speak BETTER than/WORSE than/AS WELL as (circle one) you expected you would? Why? _____

_____

PRIOR to your public speaking event (from the moment you got the assignment until you began your walk to the front of the audience), what symptoms did you experience? _____

_____

_____

DURING your speech, what symptoms did you experience? _____

_____

_____

AFTER your public speaking experience (from the moment you walked away from the audience), what symptoms did you experience? _____

_____

_____

Which symptom was strongest -- the one of which you were most aware? _____

_____

Any ideas what might have triggered this? Be as specific as possible. _____

_____

Which symptom was the least bothersome? _____

_____

Would you say your speech fright symptoms have IMPROVED/BECOME WORSE (circle one) since your previous public speaking experience? Why? _____

_____

Speech Anxiety
Follow-up Analysis

U se this form to track your speech anxiety symptoms. Complete the form as soon as possible following your public speaking experience. Share the information with your instructor or school counselor. Together you can work out a plan to minimize the symptoms.

Date of speaking event: _____ Time of speaking event: _____am/pm

Place: _____

Number of people in the audience: _____ Describe the audience: _____

_____

_____

What did you *most* like about your speech? _____

_____

What did you *least* like about your speech? _____

_____

Did you speak BETTER than/WORSE than/AS WELL as (circle one) you expected you would? Why? _____

_____

PRIOR to your public speaking event (from the moment you got the assignment until you began your walk to the front of the audience), what symptoms did you experience? _____

_____

_____

DURING your speech, what symptoms did you experience? _____

_____

_____

AFTER your public speaking experience (from the moment you walked away from the audience), what symptoms did you experience? _____

_____

_____

Which symptom was strongest -- the one of which you were most aware? _____

_____

Any ideas what might have triggered this? Be as specific as possible. _____

_____

Which symptom was the least bothersome? _____

_____

Would you say your speech fright symptoms have IMPROVED/BECOME WORSE (circle one) since your previous public speaking experience? Why? _____

_____

Speech Anxiety
Follow-up Analysis

Use this form to track your speech anxiety symptoms. Complete the form as soon as possible following your public speaking experience. Share the information with your instructor or school counselor. Together you can work out a plan to minimize the symptoms.

Date of speaking event: _____ Time of speaking event: _____am/pm

Place: _____

Number of people in the audience: _____ Describe the audience: _____

_____

_____

What did you _most_ like about your speech? _____

_____

What did you _least_ like about your speech? _____

_____

Did you speak BETTER than/WORSE than/AS WELL as (circle one) you expected you would? Why? _____

_____

PRIOR to your public speaking event (from the moment you got the assignment until you began your walk to the front of the audience), what symptoms did you experience? _____

_____

_____

DURING your speech, what symptoms did you experience? _____

_____

_____

AFTER your public speaking experience (from the moment you walked away from the audience), what symptoms did you experience? _____

_____

_____

Which symptom was strongest -- the one of which you were most aware? _____

_____

Any ideas what might have triggered this? Be as specific as possible. _____

_____

Which symptom was the least bothersome? _____

_____

Would you say your speech fright symptoms have IMPROVED/BECOME WORSE (circle one) since your previous public speaking experience? Why? _____

_____

Speech Anxiety
Follow-up Analysis

Use this form to track your speech anxiety symptoms. Complete the form as soon as possible following your public speaking experience. Share the information with your instructor or school counselor. Together you can work out a plan to minimize the symptoms.

Date of speaking event: _____ Time of speaking event: _____am/pm

Place: _____

Number of people in the audience: _____ Describe the audience: _____

_____

_____

What did you _most_ like about your speech? _____

_____

What did you _least_ like about your speech? _____

_____

Did you speak BETTER than/WORSE than/AS WELL as (circle one) you expected you would? Why? _____

_____

PRIOR to your public speaking event (from the moment you got the assignment until you began your walk to the front of the audience), what symptoms did you experience? _____

_____

_____

DURING your speech, what symptoms did you experience? _____

_____

_____

AFTER your public speaking experience (from the moment you walked away from the audience), what symptoms did you experience? _____

_____

_____

Which symptom was strongest -- the one of which you were most aware? _____

_____

Any ideas what might have triggered this? Be as specific as possible. _____

_____

Which symptom was the least bothersome? _____

_____

Would you say your speech fright symptoms have IMPROVED/BECOME WORSE (circle one) since your previous public speaking experience? Why? _____

_____

Speech Anxiety
Follow-up Analysis

U se this form to track your speech anxiety symptoms. Complete the form as soon as possible following your public speaking experience. Share the information with your instructor or school counselor. Together you can work out a plan to minimize the symptoms.

Date of speaking event: _____ Time of speaking event: _____am/pm

Place: _____

Number of people in the audience: _____ Describe the audience: _____

_____

_____

What did you _most_ like about your speech? _____

_____

What did you _least_ like about your speech? _____

_____

Did you speak BETTER than/WORSE than/AS WELL as (circle one) you expected you would? Why? _____

_____

PRIOR to your public speaking event (from the moment you got the assignment until you began your walk to the front of the audience), what symptoms did you experience? _____

_____

_____

DURING your speech, what symptoms did you experience? _____

_____

_____

AFTER your public speaking experience (from the moment you walked away from the audience), what symptoms did you experience? _____

_____

_____

Which symptom was strongest -- the one of which you were most aware? _____

_____

Any ideas what might have triggered this? Be as specific as possible. _____

_____

Which symptom was the least bothersome? _____

_____

Would you say your speech fright symptoms have IMPROVED/BECOME WORSE (circle one) since your previous public speaking experience? Why? _____

_____

Speech Anxiety
Follow-up Analysis

Use this form to track your speech anxiety symptoms. Complete the form as soon as possible following your public speaking experience. Share the information with your instructor or school counselor. Together you can work out a plan to minimize the symptoms.

Date of speaking event: _____ Time of speaking event: _____am/pm

Place: _____

Number of people in the audience: _____ Describe the audience: _____

_____

_____

What did you _most_ like about your speech? _____

_____

What did you _least_ like about your speech? _____

_____

Did you speak BETTER than/WORSE than/AS WELL as (circle one) you expected you would? Why? _____

_____

165

PRIOR to your public speaking event (from the moment you got the assignment until you began your walk to the front of the audience), what symptoms did you experience? _____

_____

_____

DURING your speech, what symptoms did you experience? _____

_____

_____

AFTER your public speaking experience (from the moment you walked away from the audience), what symptoms did you experience? _____

_____

_____

Which symptom was strongest -- the one of which you were most aware? _____

_____

Any ideas what might have triggered this? Be as specific as possible. _____

_____

Which symptom was the least bothersome? _____

_____

Would you say your speech fright symptoms have IMPROVED/BECOME WORSE (circle one) since your previous public speaking experience? Why? _____

_____

Speech Anxiety
Follow-up Analysis

U se this form to track your speech anxiety symptoms. Complete the form as soon as possible following your public speaking experience. Share the information with your instructor or school counselor. Together you can work out a plan to minimize the symptoms.

Date of speaking event: _____ Time of speaking event: _____am/pm

Place: _____

Number of people in the audience: _____ Describe the audience: _____

_____

_____

What did you _most_ like about your speech? _____

_____

What did you _least_ like about your speech? _____

_____

Did you speak BETTER than/WORSE than/AS WELL as (circle one) you expected you would? Why? _____

_____

PRIOR to your public speaking event (from the moment you got the assignment until you began your walk to the front of the audience), what symptoms did you experience? _____

_____

_____

DURING your speech, what symptoms did you experience? _____

_____

_____

AFTER your public speaking experience (from the moment you walked away from the audience), what symptoms did you experience? _____

_____

_____

Which symptom was strongest -- the one of which you were most aware? _____

_____

Any ideas what might have triggered this? Be as specific as possible. _____

_____

Which symptom was the least bothersome? _____

_____

Would you say your speech fright symptoms have IMPROVED/BECOME WORSE (circle one) since your previous public speaking experience? Why? _____

_____

Speech Anxiety
Follow-up Analysis

Use this form to track your speech anxiety symptoms. Complete the form as soon as possible following your public speaking experience. Share the information with your instructor or school counselor. Together you can work out a plan to minimize the symptoms.

Date of speaking event: _____ Time of speaking event: _____am/pm

Place: _____

Number of people in the audience: _____ Describe the audience: _____

_____

_____

What did you *most* like about your speech? _____

_____

What did you *least* like about your speech? _____

_____

Did you speak BETTER than/WORSE than/AS WELL as (circle one) you expected you would? Why? _____

_____

PRIOR to your public speaking event (from the moment you got the assignment until you began your walk to the front of the audience), what symptoms did you experience? _____

_____

_____

DURING your speech, what symptoms did you experience? _____

_____

_____

AFTER your public speaking experience (from the moment you walked away from the audience), what symptoms did you experience? _____

_____

_____

Which symptom was strongest -- the one of which you were most aware? _____

_____

Any ideas what might have triggered this? Be as specific as possible. _____

_____

Which symptom was the least bothersome? _____

_____

Would you say your speech fright symptoms have IMPROVED/BECOME WORSE (circle one) since your previous public speaking experience? Why? _____

_____